# COLLEGE WITHOUT COMPROMISE

*An Encouraging Guide to Starting Early,*
*Finishing Economically, and*
*Protecting Your Homeschool Vision*

Scott & Kris Wightman

HOMESCHOOL SAMPLER PUBLISHING
ST. LOUIS, MISSOURI
www.homeschoolsampler.com

Cover and page design by Daniel Ford

ISBN: 0-9773519-0-4

Printed in the United States of America by:
Cenveo Plus
2828 Brannon Avenue
St. Louis, MO  63139

# Contents

# *Foreword*

Wherever I go, speaking at conferences and conventions, I get questions. If we should ever meet, and you ask me a question, chances are the delay in response from me isn't that I'm trying to *determine* the right answer, but that I'm trying to *find* the right answer. I'm mentally flipping through my card catalog, looking for the answer I always give whenever I'm asked that question. If, on the other hand, my eyes grow wide, you have won the jackpot, and have come up with a question I haven't heard before.

The most common question among *non*-homeschoolers is simple enough, "What about socialization?" If "socialization" means, and it does, "the seizing of the means of production by the state," I think I'll take a pass with my kids. But the most common question among homeschoolers is this, "What about college?"

Most of today's homeschooling parents find themselves serving as a rather peculiar bridge. We were educated ourselves at government schools, but we pray our grandchildren will not only be homeschooled, but will homeschool our great-grandchildren. We're the dry land across the Red Sea. One of our greatest challenges is to get rid of the unspoken, underlying assumptions about what education is, the bathwater we brought with us to our classroom.

The good news is that even when we make this curious choice of doing school at home, it's really not that hard to do. College, at home – now that's a horse of a different color. That's why the question is so common. Do we give up our convictions in order for our child to get a college education? Do we give up our hopes for college because our convictions will get in the way? Is there one plan for our sons and another plan for our daughters? Is a Christian college three states away better than a local secular college where my child can live at home? Is a distance degree more or less valuable than the homeschool diploma we plan to print off our computers?

Like most of the hard questions, this one requires more than simple logic chopping. You cannot plug in data and wait for the right answer to pop out. These are questions of wisdom. Which is why I can think of no better people to address the issue than Scott and Kris Wightman. The Wightmans are dear friends to the Sprouls. We chose them because of their character and wisdom. They chose us because of their grace and compassion. This is a family that is a walking testimony to the grace of God, and the wisdom of His Word. And now they have tackled the subtle questions about college and the homeschooled child. They have given us in these pages not only wisdom, but hope, and joy and direction.

I am grateful to them, and for this book, not only because it will inform our own family's decisions as our children grow older, but because now, when I am asked, "What about college?" I will have on file in my brain this simple answer, "Get *College Without Compromise*. You, your children, and your grandchildren will be glad you did."

Dr. R.C. Sproul, Jr.
Director
The Highlands Study Center
Bristol, Virginia

# Acknowledgements

We would first like to thank the customers of our homeschool bookstore in St. Louis who have been a wonderful inspiration and have been living out the fruit of turning their hearts to their children and seeing their children's hearts turned to them. You cannot begin to fathom the blessing it has been to our family to witness God's hand upon His people.

Second, we wish to thank Doug Phillips and Vision Forum Ministries (www.visionforumministries.org & www.visionforum.com) for their never-ending library of material to build up the Christian home. They have been an incredible encouragement to those families seeking to honor our Lord and raise a godly army of soldiers for the expansion of the Kingdom and the preservation of the remnant. As Mr. Phillips has quoted Charles Spurgeon:

> *The man who never reads will never be read. He who never quotes will never be quoted. He who will not use the thoughts of other men's brains, proves that he has no brains of his own… My books are my tools. They also serve as my counsel, my consolation, and my comfort. They are my source of wisdom and the font of my education. They are my friends and my delights. They are my surety, when all else is awry, that I have set my confidence in the substantial things of truth and right.[1]*

Mr. Phillips' ministry at Vision Forum, including his tapes and conferences, has been an incredible blessing to us, and we are very different people because of his influence.

Third, to Dr. R.C. Sproul, Jr. (www.highlandsstudycenter.org) for making clear the true role of the church and the family's role within that church. We have learned that we, together, are the bride of Christ and we must always be working to purify that bride, presenting it beautiful to the Savior in splendor, without spot or wrinkle, holy and without blemish. We have learned that building a culture of joy, love and service will change families, change the church, and then change the world.

Fourth, to other ministries such as James McDonald's *Books on the Path* (www.booksonthepath.com) that continue to show us an ever-increasing volume of solid, meaty books on the Christian home and godly living. We also very much appreciate Mr. McDonald's labors to bring us the magazines he publishes: "Family Reformation" and "Homeschooling Today." He is a great example of one devoting his heart and soul to the restoration of the Christian home.

Fifth, to Dan Ford, author of a wonderful book describing the influence of covenants on the family, church and state entitled, *In the Name of God, Amen*, that we would commend to all. Dan also is a graphic artist, and he has graciously designed the cover and layout for this book and helped with the details of working with the printer.

Sixth, to the families of Covenant Family Church in Troy, Missouri, who have been a constant source of inspiration and fount of many blessings. How could a family ever fail while in the midst of such godly examples of Christian love, purity and graceful parenting? And an extra thank you to Allan Schwarb for his look at an early draft, and Laura Johnson for her tireless editing of the final manuscript.

Finally, to our beautiful children, Katie, Steve, Joe, Amy, Michael, Matthew, Andrew and Emily, who are the greatest of all gifts God could possibly give. You are our heritage and our reward, despite our many failings. You are all contributors to our home life and ministry, true assets in this journey. It is a wonderful thing to see you, as you grow, taking more and more initiative to love and serve others, far beyond what we ever could have asked or imagined.

# SECTION I

---

# INTRODUCTION

# CHAPTER 1

---

# FINISHING
# STRONG

We have the privilege of working in our homeschool bookstore where each day we see family after family walk through the door with beautiful, sweet, self-controlled children. They have been protected from the influences of the world, and they shine with an astonishing purity and gentleness that is just not attainable elsewhere. The investment and sacrifices of their parents have proved effectual as they have nurtured their little ones in the ways of our God. If others could see all the fruitful families we get to see, they would never doubt that their labors will reap enormous, eternal rewards.

Cotton Mather, who along with his father was a Puritan pastor of Boston's Old North Church in the late 1600s and early 1700s, and of whom George Washington referred to as the "spiritual father of America's founding fathers,"[2] wrote twenty one points to himself that he called, "A Father's Resolutions." In the preamble, he stated:

*Parents, Oh! how much ought you to be continually devising for the good of your children! Often device how to make them "wise children"; how to give them a desirable education, an education that may render them desirable; how to render them lovely and polite, and serviceable in their generation.[3]*

We have never heard a better description of what is unique about homeschooled children. We all strive to raise children that are "lovely and polite, and serviceable in their generation." We're sure family, friends, and even strangers, regularly observe these special qualities in your children.

Let's remember why we began! We began because we believed Deuteronomy 6, that it was our responsibility to train and disciple our own children, not to delegate that awesome task and privilege to any other person or institution:

*And these words that I command you today shall be on your heart. You shall teach them diligently to your children, and shall talk of them when you sit in your house, and when you walk by the way, and when you lie down, and when you rise. (Deuteronomy 6:6-7)*

We began because we believed our influence and training was far superior to that of their peers:

*Whoever walks with the wise becomes wise, but the companion of fools will suffer harm. (Proverbs 13:20)*

And we began because our vision is not just for this generation, but for many to come:

*Things that we have heard and known, that our fathers have told us. We will not hide them from their children, but tell to the coming generation the glorious deeds of the Lord, and his might, and the wonders that he has done. He established a testimony in Jacob and appointed a law in Israel, which he commanded our fathers to teach to their children, that the next generation might know them, the children yet unborn, and arise and tell them to their children, so that they should set their hope in God and not forget the works of God, but keep his commandments. (Psalm 78:3-7)*

In Dr. R.C. Sproul, Jr.'s newest book, *When You Rise Up: A Covenantal Approach to Homeschooling*, (and, by the way, the best we have ever read on why we do this crazy, countercultural, yet wonderful, beautiful, biblical homeschool thing), he says:

> *Our vision for our homeschool, for the raising of our children in the nurture and admonition of the Lord, is not something we do just because we're supposed to. Rather, it is our very vision for making manifest the kingdom of God. And that vision of the kingdom of God isn't something only for today or off at a great distance. It is this generation's changing, through the Holy Spirit's power, the hearts of the next generation, and then their changing the next generation, and the next and the next. It is generation after generation after generation of building the kingdom, growing to be more like Christ, to love him, to imitate him, to know him aright.*[4]

However, one of the most disconcerting developments in the homeschool movement in recent years has been the ever-increasing talk of putting children back in school when they reach high school. Parents are afraid their children will not be adequately prepared for college, and they would rather err on the side of less protection from worldly influences than risk one of their children not being able to compete in college and eventually the marketplace. What about transcripts? What about the ACT or SAT? What about high school lab sciences? What about calculus? What do we put on an admissions application? What about the rigors of college academics? Homeschool parents, these fears need not be! Don't ever compromise character for academics. God is faithful! We don't have to surrender one for the sake of the other.

And don't ever let anyone tell you that you are incapable of taking your children all the way through. Dr. Sproul makes another very good point:

> *The teacher need not always be superior to the student in whatever is taught. Every major-league baseball team employs at least one*

*batting coach. But there isn't a single batting coach who is a superior hitter to the people he is coaching. If he were a better hitter than the players he teaches, he would be the one playing.*[5]

Our oldest son, Steve, has taken math courses through all the algebras and trigonometry, and we most definitely have not remembered enough about those subjects to help in any meaningful way. He does the vast majority of the work on his own, and all we do is cheer him on from the sidelines.

So, the purpose of this book is to open up a wonderful, new approach to high school and college that will excite both you and your children to finish their training at home strong and victorious. You can provide your child a college degree, if that is within the vision for your family, for less time and dramatically less money. And you can begin in high school or even before.

The method we are talking about is an independent study approach that can either give you a head start with a more traditional college, making admissions much easier and usually eliminating the need for a transcript or placement tests, or it can take you all the way through. There are several higher education institutions, designed originally for the adult learner, which will grant quality, accredited degrees without the student ever setting foot on a brick-and-mortar campus. Many of these same colleges now embrace homeschoolers.

The idea begins with the concept of turning high school coursework into college credit, essentially doing high school and college at the same time. We all know much of grade school repeats itself in middle school, a good deal of middle school repeats itself in high school, and still a lot of high school repeats itself in college. The problem is that a college wants to charge you maybe $1,200 (and often much more) to teach you a course you already know or can learn more efficiently on your own. So, by beginning while still high school age, you can knock out quite a few credits before your child even reaches the traditional college age of eighteen. You can then gradually and seamlessly transition from high school to college in a very relaxed and natural manner.

You, as a parent, can instruct your high school student much better than any traditional school in your area. There is no need to feel inferior! You may be concerned because you can't present an "official" high school transcript to a prospective college, but you can provide so much more. By beginning early, you can show them completed college coursework which, according to colleges we have spoken with, is a much better judge of your child's ability to handle college-level work than the best of high school transcripts.

Then, when they are college age, having already acquired enough to be a sophomore or even junior in higher education credits, they can continue the same path, staying at home, finishing up their degree in no time. Taking the independent approach all the way through to the end, it is not unusual for a student to have their diploma in hand in less than a year after finishing high school. And the total cost is only about $6,000. Not $6,000 per year, but $6,000 total! A combination or blended approach can also be employed which utilizes both independent studies and traditional coursework, still shortening the process, drastically reducing the funds needed, but opening up a slightly broader array of degree opportunities.

While each will be examined in much greater detail later, several tools are available that will help in the accomplishment of these goals:

1) Credit by Examination – a very inexpensive and efficient way to achieve college credit through testing programs such as CLEP, DANTES, TECEP, Excelsior and AP
2) Dual Enrollment – taking courses at a local college during the junior and senior years of high school
3) Professional, Continuing Education – in fields where continuing education is available, there are also several colleges that will grant credit for that work, thereby doing college at the same time as working toward a professional designation

4) Distance Learning – while these can still be expensive, they can be a good alternative for some of the more complex subjects

5) Portfolio Assessment – attaining credit for experience or life skills already achieved

The tools are already out there. You just have to be a little creative to piece them together to match your child's situation, talents, interests, vision and specific calling. But definitely don't be intimidated. This guide will give you a great head start and point you to other resources that will help you find the best program for your student. Our prayer is that you will come away from reading this book with a refreshed and invigorated outlook on this homeschooling adventure you have chosen for your family.

You took control of your child's education already, so don't give up now. There is no better season for the child or the parents. For us, it has been the most rewarding, energizing, successful time in our family's academic life and we encourage you not to be anxious about how you are going to prepare for, and then pull off, college. As we have spoken on this topic many times to homeschool groups, the students themselves have embraced this eagerly and with a renewed purpose and energy. How exciting for them to be sixteen or seventeen years old with several college credits to their name. They gain insight and vision into what lies ahead. This motivates them to apply themselves in a new, fresh and more independent way. Everything you have trained them for begins to pay off.

This is the victory lap. The race is yours to win! Finish strong!

**ALL THE REASONS YOU STARTED CAN CONTINUE TO THE END!**

# SECTION II

---

# ALWAYS KEEPING THE END IN MIND

# CHAPTER 2

---

## CONSIDERING A
## COURSE

In an effort to further illustrate the concerns we have heard homeschool parents express as their children reach the middle school and high school years, let's look at five hypothetical families and the choices before them.

### THE MILLER FAMILY

Family number one, the Miller family, whose oldest is now in eighth grade, is beginning to worry that their child won't be able to get into a top-rated university if they stick with their homeschooling much longer. They are thinking the Harvards and Yales of the world won't be particularly interested in some Midwestern homeschooler.

The Millers are concerned about not being able to present a transcript full of rigorous study and academic achievement from a well-respected, private, college-preparatory school. As a result, they look to enroll their child in the local Christian high school that enjoys a wonderful reputation for academic excellence and whose graduates have been gracing the halls of the Ivy League for decades. And besides, how are the parents going to teach him those tough subjects like the higher maths and physics at home? At that point, the decision seems clear, and they mail in their application to the high school.

## THE WILLIAMS FAMILY

The second family is committed to going all the way through high school, sticking with homeschooling. The parents still want to be able to walk alongside their children throughout the day. They believe the Hebrew discipleship model is the biblical pattern and are concerned that high school age is still too young to withstand daily peer influences. So, they will stay the course. They, too, are concerned about not having a traditional transcript, but they decide to do their best and will try and get through the tougher courses the best they can, maybe by incorporating an occasional video course, computer-guided study or utilizing a learning center.

For college, though, the only options they are familiar with for their sophomore are to enroll in a local college as a commuter student or go off to school. They know of a Christian college about four hours away that has a good reputation, and some of their oldest child's friends have been talking about going there. It seems like a good choice because it is far enough from home for them to feel independent, but close enough to come home fairly regularly. It also should be a reasonably sheltered environment given that it is a Christian institution. The more the Williams family considers it, the more they like the idea, so they start preparing for the ACT and begin a dialogue with the admissions office.

## THE BAKER FAMILY

Our next family, whose oldest child is a junior, has also committed to finishing high school at home. However, unlike the Williams family, the Bakers are very concerned about the financial commitment of a private college. Even with some grants, they have been told it will cost nearly $100,000 per child, and they have six. The Christian college, therefore, is just not an option. But the state university is only a couple of hours away and with average grants there, this in-state public university should only be about $50,000. Maybe with some student loans and their child working part-time while on campus, they might be able to pull it off. The big-time sports are also kind of fun, and there certainly are plenty of majors to choose from. Even being a rocket scientist is an option. So, the Bakers take a tour of the campus, and, based on their conversations with the admissions counselor, they tweak their child's senior year curriculum to make sure they meet the university's requirements. Their track is set.

## THE BROWN FAMILY

This family heard through their homeschool group about an interesting way to begin accumulating college credit, while their ninth grader is still in high school, by taking a CLEP test after completion of many of the student's high school courses. They found they could garner three to six hours of credit just for taking a computerized test on something they had already learned. They understand this will allow for a great deal of credits to be amassed outside of a structured class, and at less than $25 per credit hour.

The Browns also heard that some colleges in their area offer dual enrollment classes to homeschoolers in their junior and senior years of high school. In this arrangement, the young person is able to take some of those "tougher" courses in a classroom setting at what is usually a reduced credit-hour rate. It will also provide some experience with college-level work and an opportunity to start developing a college GPA.

Their child will then, at some later time, enroll in a traditional local college and begin to take some of their course offerings, either through correspondence or in a classroom environment. Most higher education institutions require the last thirty hours to be taken through their school, but until the senior year, their student can potentially keep accumulating credits by examination, take some less expensive courses through a community college, take some distance learning courses of varying types, and maybe even apply for a few credits based on life experience.

Equipped with this latest knowledge, the Brown family begins investigating the policies of local colleges to determine how much flexibility they can allow their child for the accruing of as many credits as possible outside the classroom. The family is heartened to find several schools where this approach will work, both for dual enrollment credit while still in high school and for the allowance of a number of different categories of credit after hitting traditional college age. They tentatively pick their favorite institution, plan for which CLEP tests their student will take the rest of the high school years, begin deciding which dual enrollment classes will be taken, and if they plan well and work hard, look forward to being a college junior when most peers are only entering freshmen. And half of college will be completed for less than $3,000.

## THE JOHNSON FAMILY

This last family is thinking about taking the Brown family's approach even further. They learned recently about three accredited colleges that will grant degrees, mostly by examination, with no requirement of being in the classroom. The Johnsons have an eighth grader that is a capable, independent learner who is motivated to finish college early and get on with the rest of life. The family is not made of money and would find it quite hard to come up with any significant contribution to their child's college expenses. They also do not live in a metropolitan area and the nearest college is an hour and a half away, too far to commute. For the Johnsons, the thought of a college degree utilizing mostly credits by examination is a huge blessing. And if their child can complete a full bachelor's degree for just a few thousand dollars and in about half the time, they just want to know where to sign up.

So, they start mapping out the credits they will need for different possible degrees, and begin planning for the CLEP's their child will take over the next few years. They also try to find other families who may have already walked this road in order to glean from their experiences. This eighth grader's family is so excited that they will, after all, have the opportunity to lead their child to a degree they previously thought was out of reach.

Our main purpose in presenting these stories is to illustrate, and take a peek into the motivations for, five typical college strategies employed by homeschool families across America. The first three point to the most common methods used today, involving the sending of children to traditional four-year colleges. But the last two describe what we think is some of the most exciting, revolutionary news to hit the modern homeschool movement since it first took flight in the early 1980s. As students of the homeschool boom start hitting high school, they need a vision for their future. And if that vision includes college, there is now a way to get it done in short order and without the monetary waste of a traditional path.

From the preceding stories, there are five unfounded concerns we would like to debunk and five wonderful opportunities we would like to commend. Here are the concerns to debunk:

1) Homeschoolers Can't Get Into Prestigious Colleges –
   This is definitely not the case - even Ivy League schools welcome homeschoolers. They obviously must score very well on the ACT or SAT and show themselves to otherwise be qualified, but Harvard, for example, has been admitting homeschoolers for quite some time.

2) The "Tough" Subjects Can't Be Learned at Home –
   As Dr. Sproul has said previously, the batting coach doesn't need to be better than the hitter, and even courses a parent doesn't understand can be learned independently by a motivated student. There are many sources of help for the independent learner in case it is needed and the student doesn't need to leave home to master difficult subjects.

3) They Might Miss the Camaraderie of Christian Peers –
Just because a higher education institution has Christian in the name or creed, doesn't mean it will be a good environment for our children. In fact, it can be worse because it has the potential for our sons and daughters to let down their guards and feel that if other Christians are doing it, they should feel comfortable doing it also.

4) They Will Miss the Fun of a Big-College Experience –
We hear this objection quite regularly, but please don't let the missing of the college "experience" woo you into making a poor decision. If we really stop and think about it, most of the college experience is irresponsible at best and reckless and destructive at worst.

5) The Independent Study Approach Offers Limited Majors –
While the purely independent study approach given in the last story does offer a limited number of majors (although one institution offers more than a hundred), by blending the methods you can still achieve much of the benefits of independent study without having any limits on the degrees available. In other words, you can begin with independent study and then transfer credits to a regular college later for the purpose of finishing up there.

On the other side, here are the opportunities of a purely independent study approach (getting almost an entire degree through credit by examination), or a combination or blended model:

1) Much Less Cost –
We will explore this in greater depth later, but the cost savings is unbelievable! Only $6,000 for the purely independent study approach versus national averages of $68,000 for in-state public universities, $103,000 for out-of-state publics, and $145,000 for private colleges and universities (these numbers

reflect current national averages and are inflated through 2009 for a student beginning the fall of 2005). This means you would be paying 11 times more, 17 times more, or 24 times more, respectively.

2) Much Less Time –
As stated earlier, these degrees can be achieved in a fraction of the time, because each student can move at his or her own pace and not be slowed down by a class. We have a good friend who earned an entire bachelor's degree in ten months, start to finish.

3) Probably Avoid High School Transcripts and Admissions Tests –
Because the student will have already achieved sophomore, or maybe even junior, status by the time he is traditional college age, he becomes a transfer student in the eyes of the university. So, there is no need for a high school transcript or for taking the ACT or SAT.

4) Provide a Means for the Tougher Courses, If Necessary –
Enrolling your student part time in a local college while he is still in high school (called dual enrollment) can be a great way for him to take his lab sciences or higher math that you may not be comfortable teaching at home. Now, we don't see any reason to fear the harder courses in your regular homeschool curriculum, but if you want some help and want your child to knock out some college credit in the process, you don't need to abandon your vision to do it.

5) Continue a Very Flexible and "Serviceful" Lifestyle –
Having a child go away to college completely disrupts the family and pulls that young person out of your family's ministry of service to others. If there would be a unique reason

for him or her to be gone, or when the time is right to be given in marriage, that is completely different. But, far too often, children go away simply because everyone else does, and that is a very poor decision-making methodology.

## THE PATH THAT HAS BEEN CLEARED

We can't help but notice that our Lord is continually opening up exciting, new avenues for our homeschoolers. As the movement matures and more and more young people are reaching ages where these decisions are upon them, God has been opening doors through His Spirit and through the work of His saints. He continues to care for the needs of His children and to illumine our paths.

When we began homeschooling back in the late 1980s, there were not very many of us around. And our family was several years behind the real pioneers who had to take on the schools, the National Education Association, and the state to win the right to teach their children at home. It's amazing that it was ever necessary to battle with our own government to gain acknowledgement of such a fundamental right, but it had to be done. We are eternally grateful for the perseverance and courage of these families who have handed us this incredible gift we now hold.

In the beginning, we didn't know how far we could go with homeschooling, because we had not yet met anyone who had finished the course. We just took it one day and one year at a time. One of the early, most popular philosophies was to homeschool just through the primary grades in order to get the kids grounded and then assume you would later place them in middle or high school. When we first started, this is what we planned to do.

This way of thinking changed gradually for us and many others. The pioneers were out ahead of us again finding more and more curriculum and working hard to change the perception of the culture, making homeschooling a completely acceptable and common option.

This change in perception has now kicked the doors of the higher education community wide open for us.

It's hard to believe, but we have a high school graduate of our own now and have learned many lessons along the way. We also have had the privilege of watching the college paths our store customers and other friends have chosen and how those have flourished. Watching their journeys has taught us so much. We are now thrilled to get their wisdom into your hands. What we are offering is not necessarily brand new, but certainly is not widely known. We hope to be part of getting the vision out.

To encourage you even a little further, through our own family's research we became friends with an admissions director at a local private college. We spoke alongside him once at a homeschool group meeting on higher education. He stated that he had been asked to speak several times at university admissions conferences on how to attract homeschoolers to their institutions. He was eager to encourage us that schools nationwide are seeking homeschool students and are actually developing business plans to recruit them.

So, draw courage from those who have walked the path before us, and know that you can do the same!

*And the Lord will guide you continually and satisfy your desire in scorched places and make your bones strong. (Isaiah 58:11a)*

# CHAPTER 3

---

# FAITH, PURITY,
# CHARACTER & SERVANTHOOD

Now that you know there is a path available for your children where they can begin college in high school and potentially stay at home throughout their college career, what are some of the spiritual considerations involved in making a wise decision for your family? Remember that before beginning any journey, you will be much more successful if you have the end in mind before you start. We have heard Doug Phillips, President of Vision Forum, quote two of his father's favorite maxims, "It is not our job to accept reality; it is our job to define it," and "Choose, don't settle."[6]

In the present case of training and discipling our children through homeschooling, the ultimate end must be our child's love and service to our Lord. If school can be polluting from kindergarten through twelfth grade, doesn't it also have the potential to be harmful in college? For those of us who went away to a traditional college, we can all attest to the impurity, lack of supervision, and lack of moral standards within those hallowed halls.

Therefore, as parents, we must seriously consider the possible harm to those still under our care if we should send them out of town to a college to sit under potentially godless mentors and commune in the constant companionship of fools. Michael Farris, President of the Homeschool Legal Defense Association, once said that he refused to pour out his heart and soul into the raising of his girls in the fear and admonition of the Lord just to let them marry a spiritual midget. We think the same principle applies here. We can't, without due deliberation and anguished prayer, send our children to the wolves for the sake of a piece of parchment and in the name of higher education. A friend recently was commenting on the fact that our culture has accepted as absolutely orthodox the idea of sending our kids off to college with no consideration of the alternatives or of the ramifications. And for that privilege we freely give those institutions the hearts and minds of our young men and women, not to mention a great deal of our money.

We are not saying that going away to college is always wrong under all circumstances. There could be situations where you feel it is right for your family. What we are saying is that great pause should be taken before making such a potentially dangerous decision. If you or your spouse personally went away to school, think of what went on in the dorm, fraternity or sorority. Recall what was taught in that weird philosophy class or in comparative religions. Think of what made certain students popular. Think of the deviant behavior. Now consider that it has likely gotten much worse since you went away. The incredible lack of protection your children would be dealing with is a lot to consider. And not only is it possible for your children themselves to fall into sin, but it is quite probable they would be in a place of living through things better left unexperienced, especially while still under your care.

One of our favorite books, *Home-Making*, was written by J.R. Miller, a pastor from the middle to late nineteenth century. In it he presents a wonderful picture of how a family can grow in gentle love and service for each other and for God. When speaking about what we parents want for our children, Miller captures it better than anyone I have ever heard:

> *But in the heart of every true Christian parent there glows an ideal of very fair beauty of character and nobleness of soul, which he wants to see his child attain. It is a vision of the most exalted life, lovelier than that which fills the thought of any sculptor as he*

*stands before his marble and begins to hew at the block; fairer than that which rises in the poet's soul as he bows in ecstatic fervor over his page. Every true, godly parent dreams of the most perfect manhood and womanhood for his children. He wants to see them grow up into Christlikeness, spotless in purity, rich in all the graces, with character fully developed and rounded out in symmetrical beauty, shining in this world, but shining more and more unto the perfect day.[7]*

Don't let them go too soon and risk losing any part of their souls to the world. Colleges are designed to influence the young minds that come through their doors, but not all is good, and it is your responsibility to keep such great temptations at a distance.

If normal adult life was like it is in school, we wouldn't be such strong advocates that children aren't normally ready for a life out on their own at eighteen. But college is not real life. The idle time, peer dependence, and access to new and more destructive temptations are not part of normal adult life, and if those things can be passed over, why not? We say the same thing about homeschooling in the primary and secondary grades. If adult life was comprised of bullying, verbal assaults, popularity contests, and temptations beyond our current wisdom and maturity, we might be persuaded by the argument that we are overly sheltering our children. (By the way, don't ever let anyone tell you sheltering is a bad word. We think it is a beautiful word and one of our greatest parental duties.)

Fortunately, for most of us, adult life is not filled with the same types of stresses and temptations the children of our culture must endure in school. And, if nothing else, we are old enough to discern them and react in a more mature way. For the most part, adults treat each other with much greater civility than children treat each other. Of course, we can all think of examples of adults that sometimes act like children, but overall we think the point is valid. We don't need to put them in compromising, unprotected situations thinking we are giving them training for the "real world." That's nonsense. It is very common for parents today to think it is right and proper to make sure their children can fend for themselves, even in the earliest years, against forces much stronger than most can withstand.

In his book, *Homeschooling: The Right Choice*, Christopher Klicka states that "in 1940 the top discipline offenses, according to educators, were talking, chewing gum, making noise, running in the halls, getting out of turn in line, wearing improper clothing, and not putting paper in wastebaskets."[8] In contrast, a 1997 government report showed several areas where principals had stated they experienced student discipline problems. The discipline issues that more than twenty percent of the principals observed, and here ranked from the most prevalent to the least, included: student tardiness, physical conflicts among students, student absenteeism/class cutting, verbal abuse of teachers, vandalism of school property, robbery or theft of items over $10, student tobacco use, student drug use, trespassing, racial tensions, student alcohol use, gangs, and student possession of weapons.[9]

So, with the goal in mind of getting our sons and daughters all the way to the finish line, and not abdicating this awesome task to anyone else, let's look at four spiritual aspects of what we want for them and see how college choices can bear on our ability to continue helping them along the narrow way.


## FAITH

We are sure that no one reading this book would disagree that the main goal in the raising of our children is to pass on our faith. What, then, are the challenges awaiting them in a traditional college? A recent Washington Post article cited a study based on a 1999 survey of 1,643 full-time faculty at 183 four-year schools in the Unites States. The authors of the study, political science professors from three prominent colleges, stated that 72 percent of those teaching at American universities and colleges described themselves as liberal and only 15 percent as conservative. That's nearly five times as many liberals. At the more elite schools, 87 percent were liberal and 13 percent conservative. By contrast, in a 1984 study, only 39 percent described themselves as liberal.

The article also pointed out that while nearly three-fourths of college professors are liberal, a 2004 Harris poll concluded that only one-third of the general public described themselves as such. And this liberalness of professors further manifests itself in their views on the favoring of abortion rights (84 percent), believing homosexuality is acceptable (67 percent), and the fact that they want the government to ensure full employment (65 percent).[10]

We believe concerns over the views of those teaching our next generation gets even more dangerous when we consider that in college they are in an almost completely unsupervised environment, often many miles from home, and with their peers ready and willing to jump in and reinforce unbiblical ideas. We must exercise extreme caution anytime we voluntarily subject our children to the teaching of others, but with these sobering study results in hand, we cannot afford to ignore the realities.

*Blessed is the man who walks not in the counsel of the wicked, nor stands in the way of sinners, nor sits in the seat of scoffers; but his delight is in the law of the Lord, and on his law he meditates day and night. (Psalm 1:1-2)*

Dr. Brian Ray, President of the National Home Education Research Institute, recently published a book entitled, *Home Educated and Now Adults*. The book presents the results of his 2003 study of young adults who were homeschooled and are now in adult life. His study states that 94 percent of the 5,254 people surveyed agree that their religious beliefs as adults are basically the same as their parents.[11] By contrast, recent studies have shown 75 to 85 percent of Christian youth who were raised in the church but attended public schools, renounce their faith and/or quit going to church within two years after high school graduation.[12] Something goes on when children are left to the unprotected teaching of others. It doesn't normally go as planned.

By the way, another very encouraging statistic from Dr. Ray's book is that 95 percent of homeschoolers are glad they were homeschooled[13] and only four percent don't plan to homeschool their own children.[14]

We must nurture and protect our children's faith, and if we hand over any aspect of their training to others, it must be done with fear, trembling and a great deal of due diligence. As we all know, many higher education institutions and professors believe their main goal is not to educate the young people of our society in the practical knowledge necessary to pursue a career, but rather to indoctrinate them into thinking like a "global citizen." They would describe the goal as helping their students to think "rightly", but we know what it really means is that they want them to think "leftly".

I (Scott) had to take a philosophy course while attending a state university. I opted for logic, because it sounded less touchy-feely than some of the other offerings. What a shock! While we did learn some of the discipline like, "If A equals B and B equals C, then A equals C", the rest of the course was just babble and a free form discussion of how to piece life together without God. And this was back when only 39 percent of college professors were liberal, versus today's 72 percent.

Are Christian colleges a safe alternative? Do they provide adequate protection for the faith of our children? Based on some of our own experiences and the experiences of some we know well, our personal opinion is that you still must remain guarded. We have seen examples of class assignments and required reading that would seriously disappoint any committed believer.

However, our goal in writing this book is not to make decisions for any family, only to warn of the potential dangers. There may be a Christian college that would serve your family's needs well while still enabling you to protect the vision you are working so hard to pass down. Just don't let your guard down simply because an institution waves the Christian banner. Stay wise and discerning.

## PURITY

This section almost doesn't need to be written. We all know the dangers and temptations in the world that seem to be concentrated even more intensely on college campuses. We believe the young men and women of our culture are not ready to experience unsupervised, unaccountable living at such an early age, and there are consequences if we allow it to happen. Everything we have protected them from through high school is now at their disposal. And I guess we aren't even as concerned about our children becoming the initiators of the recklessness, but rather being the victims of being led to the slaughter. We must take very seriously whether or not they have the strength to stand up under it as they are desensitized by it all day every day for four years.

I (Scott) worked for a university for five years. In my capacity, I saw all the liability claims against the institution brought by the student body alleging abuse by other students. Assault, rape, date rape, druggings, harassment, stalking; all are part of the "campus experience" that for some strange reason has been made an almost mandatory part of our culture's passage to adulthood. And it's not just what might happen to them personally, but what they see and hear and feel. Do we really want our children to be living in a situation where they will look back on those days with shame and discomfort?

A secular book released earlier this year called *Binge, What Your College Student Won't Tell You: Campus Life in an Age of Disconnection and Excess*,[15] reveals, more graphically than we were ready for, what really goes on in residence halls across America. The author, a reporter for *Time* magazine and trustee at Hamilton College in New York, spent time in the dorms of twelve prestigious universities over the course of two years, and portrays campus life as satiated with completely uncommitted physical relationships, unchecked alcohol and drug use, and as an incubator for depression and despair.

He puts much of the blame on the administration's focus of attracting students, and then their resultant misguided policies. Just looking at the complete acceptability of co-ed dorms, and now even co-ed floors and bathrooms, should be a very serious warning to us as to how far things have deteriorated.

What in the world are we thinking? We have to assume that the administration wants the young men and women to begin breaking down the barriers to a fully integrated society where there are no differences between male and female. What a huge, misguided mistake; one in which the consequences are far-reaching. Their goal of social justice may be admired among their colleagues, but they fail to acknowledge the potential for victims in this dangerous experiment.

*Finally, brothers, whatever is true, whatever is honorable, whatever is just, whatever is pure, whatever is lovely, whatever is commendable, if there is any excellence, if there is anything worthy of praise, think about these things. What you have learned and received and heard and seen in me--practice these things, and the God of peace will be with you. (Philippians 4:8-9)*

Keep your children pure! Continue to provide for them a pure, lovely, loving, joyful, safe, God-fearing place to live until you send them out for the purpose of beginning a home of their own.

We mentioned Cotton Mather's Resolutions in the Introduction, and his fourteenth applies here.

*I will be very watchful and cautious about the companions of my children. I will be very inquisitive what company they keep; if they are in hazard of being ensnared by any vicious company, I will earnestly pull them out of it, as brands out of the burning. I will find out, and procure, laudable companions for them.[16]*

It is our responsibility, parents, to be the protectors of our children and see that role through to the end.

Another of our favorite books is by a nineteenth century pastor named William Sprague. He lost his wife, and then purposed to write several beautiful letters to his daughter. Compiled, the book is entitled *Letters on Practical Subjects to a Daughter*. One of his letters is on the topic of education, and we love his words:

> *I cannot close this letter without again reminding you that, as an accountable and immortal creature, you are to regard all other kinds of improvement as subordinate to the culture of the heart; and that your acquisitions, if they are not sanctified by divine grace, will ultimately prove a curse to you rather than a blessing. While I am earnestly desirous that you should make the most of your opportunities for improving your mind, I confess that I am not without apprehension lest you should neglect the one thing needful; and more than that, lest you should find temptations to the neglect of it growing out of circumstances connected with your education. If you have strong relish for study, there is danger that study will become with you the all-engrossing concern, and will leave you without any thoughts to bestow upon God or your soul's salvation. There is danger too, that in your daily and accidental intercourse with thoughtless companions, you will contract the same habit of indifference to religion which you witness in them, and this habit will soon become fortified by the powerful influence of example, and the dread of being singular.*[17]

Dr. Sprague powerfully shows us the dangers of putting education first, to the detriment of your child's relationship with his or her Savior, and illustrates how the spending of too much time with godless peers can influence an otherwise faithful young person. Our culture puts so much pressure on our youth to fit in that the thought of standing alone, or "being singular" as Dr. Sprague puts it, proves often to be more than they can bear.

He says you must recognize the dangers of finding "temptations to the neglect of [the heart] growing out of circumstances connected with your education." Education is good and noble, but even in the

1800s, the peripherals surrounding the education system were a real danger. We once had a school superintendent tell us, "We try and do our best to teach children the ABC's, give them sound math skills, and introduce them to the social and natural sciences, but the real education happens on the bus." We're afraid that statement is all too true. It's not the reading, writing and arithmetic we fear, it's everything else that comes with it.

## CHARACTER

Character is another issue. If your child is away, there will be plenty of temptation to cut corners and follow the crowd. Especially at large universities, cheating is a way of life. Before I (Scott) was a believer, I was in a fraternity at a large state university. Cheating schemes were a way of life in our house. Preparation for tests centered on finding a person to cheat off of. Term paper assignments meant locating (often buying) a previously written paper.

One day I was walking past a friend's room, and he had two open books on his desk spread quite far apart, one on the right and one on the left, with nothing in between. I asked him what he was doing, and he said he was studying. I said, "Why are the books so far apart?" He said he wasn't studying the content of the books but was practicing straining his eyes so he could read the words with his peripheral vision. The next morning he wanted to be able to read the test papers of the students on each side.

And, sadly, it is not just secular schools that have this problem. A Christian university recently announced that it was changing its honor code after an anonymous survey revealed 47 percent of students admitted to having cheated. The old code relied on a student's own principles and other students' sense of integrity to turn in cheaters. The new code is designed "to take the burden away from the students and place it more squarely with the faculty member in his or her class." Professors will be required to discuss cheating and its implications, and they will no longer be allowed to leave the room during an examination.[18]

As with homeschooling in the earlier grades, one of the wonderful advantages we have over the traditional school environment is that the character they catch will be ours. Now that certainly can be a scary thought, and a sobering one, but we're assuming our influence will far outweigh the pressures of their peers and professors.

## SERVANTHOOD

In Mather's Preamble, he states that he is dreaming and scheming of how to give his children:

*...a desirable education, an education that may render them desirable; how to render them lovely and polite, and serviceable in their generation.*[19]

We want our children to be desirable to others, to be lovely and polite, and to be "serviceable." Do traditional colleges teach these things? Not usually. Some may have service projects and some Christian colleges may even have evangelism or missions trips, but are they really teaching the students to have a servant's heart? There are so many distractions when it comes to institutional service projects like this. We need to focus on the motives, and make sure we are not teaching them to serve only in front of man or only when someone else plans it. Or only when they heard that really cute guy or girl is going to be there.

The type of servanthood our children should strive to attain is that of finding ways to do things for others when no one is looking, when there is nothing to gain for themselves, and which flows from the heart. This surrendering to serve our Lord is what will "render them desirable," helping them grow into caring, sharing, godly adults.

Where is the best place to learn these lessons and to begin living out a life of service? The home, of course. We can be working together as a family, all while the older children are still there to model their servant's hearts for the younger ones.

Consider what great employees, husbands and fathers your sons will be, and what great wives and mothers your daughters will be as they keep this homeschool vision alive all the way until they're ready to establish homes of their own. What great ministries their new homes will have as they have learned from you how to serve, and have practiced it over and over.

In the end, we will have created a "normalness" for them that will live on under their own initiative. This is the stuff multigenerational faithfulness is built upon.

*For I have chosen [Abraham], that he may command his children and his household after him to keep the way of the Lord by doing righteousness and justice, so that the Lord may bring to Abraham what he has promised him. (Genesis 18:19)*

# CHAPTER 4

---

# HELP WANTED:
# MUST BE WILLING TO WORK

We wrote this chapter while on a family vacation, and as we were driving through Southern Illinois we couldn't help but notice a sign on an automotive repair shop. It stated, "Help Wanted: Must Be Willing to Work." While we assume it was meant to be funny, which we thought it was, it is all too true in our society that work is no longer a virtue. Work has become something to be avoided at all costs, or at least only engaged in when absolutely necessary.

So, the purpose of this chapter is to encourage you that if you are raising your children, as most homeschoolers are, to enjoy and appreciate hard work, you have no idea how far ahead of the game you already are. When your children go out into the marketplace to begin their careers, they will be competing against the MTV generation. While we haven't researched the subject ourselves, something tells us that Snoop Dogg probably is not extolling the virtues of honest labor.

Even our government seems quite pleased to promote a get-rich-quick mentality. When the lottery was first introduced in Missouri the advertisements went something like, "Win mega-millions, get crazy, stinkin', filthy rich and rub it in the faces of all your friends, and never lift a finger again." And then they would follow with a ridiculous disclaimer, "This message is not meant to be an inducement to play the lottery." Well, it obviously *was* meant to be an enticement to get something for nothing, and it has further promoted this cultural slide we are experiencing.

It's not as though no one else works hard, but it is our observation that it's often done with selfish motives. People aren't stupid. They know that in order to live a high lifestyle some dues will have to be paid, but it's often with selfish motivation. Hopefully, we are instilling in our children the biblical notion of "working unto the Lord." This is where our work ethic should come from. And the result, after practicing this over a long period of time in our homes, will be success. We recently saw a quote from Horace Greeley, and while he wasn't necessarily a man to admire, we like one of his sayings: "The darkest hour in any man's life is when he sits down to plan how to get money without earning it."

> *Now we command you, brothers, in the name of our Lord Jesus Christ, that you keep away from any brother who is walking in idleness and not in accord with the tradition that you received from us. For you yourselves know how you ought to imitate us, because we were not idle when we were with you, nor did we eat anyone's bread without paying for it, but with toil and labor we worked night and day, that we might not be a burden to any of you. It was not because we do not have that right, but to give you in ourselves an example to imitate. For even when we were with you, we would give you this command: If anyone is not willing to work, let him not eat. (2 Thessalonians 3:6-10)*

Many homeschoolers share with us their quiet insecurities about the unknown future that lies ahead for their children. Because we are raising one of the first generations to be educated at home, we often doubt ourselves and question whether our children will be received into the workforce without reservation. But the answer is a resounding YES! In Dr. Ray's study, 92 percent believe being homeschooled is an advantage to them as an adult[20] and only two percent believe being homeschooled has limited their career choices.[21]

Be assured that they would be successful if only because the competition is so weak. Most young men and women in our culture are more focused on the next party and the newest fad than on preparing for their future. But without the baggage of the school environment that promotes self-absorption, entertainment and celebrity, we know that your children will do so much better than just passing on the curve. They truly will be assets to their employers or even successful entrepreneurs.

Character is everything. They will succeed because they will know how to apply themselves. Their bosses can have complete trust in them. Employers delight in employees who work hard and make their lives easier. If we have trained them to work unto the Lord and honor those in authority the way Scripture admonishes us, we can be confident they will stand out -- way out!

American businesses struggle to find competent employees. A common cry from employers is the workforce's lack of basic educational skills and the dramatic decline of moral integrity. Colleges are no different. They, too, must work with the quality of students that are being educated in today's system. Remember they are businesses, also. In order for them to remain in business, they must offer remedial classes just to get their students up to speed and keep the tuition rolling in. According to the most recent data from the National Center for Education Statistics, in the fall of 2000, 20 percent of entering freshmen at four-year public institutions and 42 percent at community colleges had to take a remedial course.[22]

Since our store opened, we have had the opportunity to meet many local college professors. One of them was teaching remedial math at a community college, and he had cited statistics similar to those above. In fact, his were much worse -- we were very surprised. He said his college offered both a remedial math course and a remedial, remedial course. He went on to say that the first teaches at the seventh- through ninth-grade level and the second at the fifth- and sixth-grade level. But the good news is that he had never had a homeschooler in his class, though we know many are enrolled in the college. Whatever you may feel day to day, homeschooling does work!

Other local professors have also come in to encourage us, but one was just plain curious. The curious one has become my (Kris') favorite so far. During his first visit he wandered around quietly, just looking over these families who had decided to take on such a questionable venture. I then saw him observe our children, watching them interact with some of the customers.

Eventually, he approached a few of our grade school children and proceeded to engage them in conversation. I watched them from the side as he quizzed them about their studies. I knew what he was looking for. Could they socialize? This is always the paramount question that onlookers are puzzled by the most. Like most other homeschooled children, our children interacted with this gentleman like they did with anyone else. They confidently answered his questions with both cheerfulness and eye contact.

Afterwards, he came up to the counter and told me that he recently has had many homeschool students in his college class. He said he is fascinated by them and wanted me to shed light on what makes them tick. He said they seem unaware of the social demands around them and instead stay focused on their studies. He also asked the same question the majority of other visiting professors have asked as well, "Why are they always ahead of me in the book?" It seems that a lot of homeschooled students approach their professors before, during and after class with questions about their textbook, but in chapters that have not yet been covered.

This particular man had been a math professor for over thirty years, and he said that working ahead in the book had never been a problem in the past. But it was happening over and over again now with his homeschooled students. I had to explain to him, like other professors before him, that they do not have bad intentions. They have just not grown up in an environment where they have to wait for the rest of the group. They think it is normal to master a subject at their own pace. After exchanging a few friendly stories he left, smiling and less confused. Much to our enjoyment, he has sent a few messages back to our store through homeschooling families. One was, "Tell the families that come in that last semester's highest ranking math student was a dual-enrolled, fourteen-year-old homeschool student."

The vast majority of students are not getting a better education in today's school system than you are giving your children. And our nation invested over $8,041 per student per year in 2002-03, $455 billion in total;[23] all while our functional illiteracy rate hovers around 20 percent[24] and 15 percent of our adult population does not finish high school.[25]

We can't heap all the blame at the feet of the schools, though. We understand that, after all, they too must work with what they get, and there are so many families today in crisis and other families completely unengaged in their children's lives. Teachers are overwhelmed with issues that were unheard of years ago. There are many noble teachers trying to keep their fingers in the dikes, trying to keep things from getting worse, but it often seems like a losing battle.

So, if you apply yourself to teaching your children biblical values, a strong work ethic, and selfless character, as well as work to give them a solid academic foundation, they will succeed. And yes, employers will notice and fight to get them.

> *Therefore, my beloved brothers, be steadfast, immovable, always abounding in the work of the Lord, knowing that in the Lord your labor is not in vain. (1 Corinthians 15:58)*

# CHAPTER 5

---

## PROVIDING FOR A
## SINGLE INCOME HOUSEHOLD

We begin this topic with the assumption that we all want to pass down the gift of homeschooling for many, many generations. That being said, we also understand it is probably tougher to be a successful homeschool family when both parents work outside the home. We certainly know families who are in unusual circumstances, and are making the best of it with God's grace, but I think we would agree that our sons should plan to be the principal provider for their future homes.

Because both theory and practice are important, we are splitting this chapter into two parts. First, we will discuss the implanting of this vision into our sons early on to assure they are dreaming of it and planning for it. Second, we offer some practical considerations that might help the dream become a reality in your sons' lives.

### IMPLANTING THE VISION

Are your sons longing for the day when they will be established in homes of their own? Do they desire a godly marriage and look forward to raising the next generation? This is one of their principal callings, and they need to prepare early for this next season of life. Will some be single and some not be able to have children? Of course the answer is yes. However, most of them will be heads of households some day and it would be foolish not to plan for that likely scenario.

As Deuteronomy 6 instructs, we should be seizing opportunities as we sit in our house, when we walk by the way, when we lie down, and when we rise, to pump them up for the thrilling call of family leadership. Our culture needs family reformation so badly, and we, along with our sons, need to be playing a key role in bringing that reformation about. We need to be cooperating with God in turning the hearts of our children to us. And then our sons, in response, will have hearts that are turned to their children. It all flows beautifully from parent to child, and then it naturally flows from that child to his own children. This is God's desire for families as they seek to honor and serve Him.

> *Great is the Lord, and greatly to be praised, and his greatness is unsearchable. One generation shall commend your works to another, and shall declare your mighty acts. On the glorious splendor of your majesty, and on your wondrous works, I will meditate. They shall speak of the might of your awesome deeds, and I will declare your greatness. They shall pour forth the fame of your abundant goodness and shall sing aloud of your righteousness. (Psalm 145:3-7)*

Obviously, a major part of leading a home is providing for a home, and that is where we now focus. Our culture seems to put either too much emphasis or not enough on bringing home the bacon, but we think the biblical answer lies in between. We know the rich fool put too much importance on his riches, and we know we cannot serve two masters, both God and money. But, at the same time, he who does not provide for his own family is worse than an unbeliever. So, the answer lies in teaching your sons they must provide for their families, but the pursuit of affluence must never become what drives them. The income they pursue needs to be for the purpose of supplying the needs of their family and having the ability to help others that God may put in their path.

It's not as though a man's occupation is just a means to an end, either, because that can be a dangerous philosophy. A father can have an impact on many people through his profession. Much of his personal ministry may end up being through the reaching and teaching of those he comes in contact with at work. He can be a pleasing and fragrant aroma, living out a life committed to his Creator while in the marketplace. We hope that each husband and father reading this book can see the purposes in his being planted where he is, and then see his role in passing this vision to his sons.

A second reason that work is not simply a means to an end is that the idea of taking dominion is a biblical one, and building a career or building a family business for the glory of God can be a high calling. The world needs most of the products it creates. Our neighbors need power, water, food, clothing and shelter. Our friends need automobiles. Our church needs books, paper and computers. These are all good things, and the saints' contributions to our economy are far-reaching and, we believe, pleasing to our Lord. God has placed His image in us, and part of that image is to create and build.

The final reason our professions are not simply a means to an end is that God appreciates, encourages and commands us to work. Work is good! It was planned from the beginning, even before Adam's fall.

*The Lord God took the man and put him in the garden of Eden to work it and keep it. (Genesis 2:15)*

Was the original vision of work distorted somewhat after the fall? Certainly, yes. But, the curse was not on the work itself. The punishment was simply that the work would be more difficult and more toilsome. It was still meant to be worthy and good. One of the worst things we could do to our sons is make them think work is a curse and something to be avoided. This philosophy will only lead them to be dissatisfied, grumpy and complaining, and this makes for a lousy husband and father.

So how does this relate to school work? School is both a necessary preamble to a career and a training ground for learning the value of, and proper attitude toward, work. But the vision we want to encourage here is that if your sons desire to be leaders of their homes someday, they can begin to learn to see that their labors in school have a purpose. They fit within the overall plan and can be embraced as good and lovely, rather than seen as a nuisance and irritant.

As our oldest son progresses through high school and has also been accumulating many college credits in the process, he more and more sees the role of school within his desire for a godly family of his own. He sees that his educational labors now will be respected by his future wife and help provide for the needs of his children. You wives can only begin to realize the joy it brings a husband to know he is honorable in your eyes and is being a good example for your children. Husbands, you know well the reward of fulfilling your God-given role. The point is that you are missing a beautiful opportunity with your son if you are not connecting the dots for him and helping him to see that his extra efforts now will make him better at fulfilling his role later. His labors now will directly help earn the gratitude of his future wife. His mastering of algebra now will actually help garner the esteem of his children.

Ask your sons. See if this might energize them to use the high school years as a wonderful season of training and preparation and not a season of purposelessness, self-absorption and folly. Just go to the mall any Saturday night and see what your sons are not to become. The contrast is easy to find. It is all around us. Just look at the emptiness in their eyes. Their world is not one of reality, but one of popularity and fitting in. They live for today alone with their "whatever" attitudes.

*What do I gain if, humanly speaking, I fought with beasts at Ephesus? If the dead are not raised, "Let us eat and drink, for tomorrow we die." Do not be deceived: "Bad company ruins good morals." (1 Corinthians 15:32-33)*

Nothing really matters to them except the current struggle to survive in their artificial world of popularity, slander and recklessness. It's almost impossible for them to focus on their future, because today is too hard, too painful, too hopeless.

Providing for a single-income family is a high calling. It is sometimes a tough calling, though, in today's economy. Large purchases, especially, are bid up by double-income households. Nevertheless, it is a calling we must hold on to and see as one of our primary roles, as we prepare our sons for this great adventure.

Everyone has heard of DINK's: Double Income No Kids. And we heard another one recently: SITCOM's, which stands for Single Income Two Children Oppressive Mortgage. But we are proud to be SILK's: Single Income Lots of Kids. If you want your sons to be SILK's, and even avoid that oppressive mortgage, you'll need to walk with them and help them define their path.

It is our responsibility to help establish them in a vocation. The last two sentences of another of Cotton Mather's Resolutions, speaking of a father preparing his children to earn a living, states:

> *The children of the best fashion, may have occasion to bless the parents that make such a provision for them! The Jews have a saying worth remembering: "Whoever doesn't teach his son some trade or business, teaches him to be a thief."*[26]

## PRACTICAL THOUGHTS

As promised, we will now move beyond theory into application. How should our sons best prepare themselves to fulfill this high calling?

The most obvious consideration would have to be the picking of a profession to pursue. The substance of the deliberation is, in our mind, fivefold:

1) Is it a profession that can support a family on one income?
2) Does it have the potential to grow as a family grows?

3) Can the skills and/or relationships involved in the profession be passed down to the next generation?

4) Could the skills and/or relationships be turned into a family business some day?

5) Is the profession noble and pure?

### Is it a profession that can support a family on one income?

Unfortunately, not all professions reasonably support a family on one income. What level of income is necessary, obviously, depends on where your sons plan to live and the lifestyle their new families might expect to sustain. Cost of living can vary widely across the country and from cities to rural areas. Also, your family may be used to a certain standard of living and your children need to decide whether they want to keep that standard when they establish their own homes.

Some of these decisions will come with thought, prayer and intense deliberation, while some will come by default in the absence of a plan. It is always a virtue to be good stewards of the resources God has given, and diligence should certainly be given to living on less. Otherwise, uncontrolled debt will likely be the result, and future plans to invest in something entrepreneurial will be limited.

Is a white-collar job necessary? Is college a requirement? Can a job in the trades bring in the income needed? Is there the potential to move into management or ownership later? We obviously can't answer these questions for you, nor would we want to presume we might know what is best for your sons. The point, however, is not that there are strict right and wrong answers, but that there should be a great deal of consideration and the seeking of God's will should be pursued.

This is an area where the principle of talking about these things with your son "when you sit in your house, and when you walk by the way, and when you lie down, and when you rise" would be extremely valuable. Decisions such as these take time, and they need to roll around. Our family likes to try thoughts on for a time and talk them through thoroughly. What profession to explore is weighty and the preparations vary widely, so it is important to start early.

If college ends up being part of the plan, though, don't forget that later in the book we will be outlining a blueprint for making it go much quicker and cost much less. College isn't for everyone, but it no longer needs to be a mountain that can't be climbed without serious debt. Establishing a new home without debt means the options are much broader. And it will take a lot less income to support your son's new family if student loans aren't part of the picture.

**Does it have the potential to grow as a family grows?**

A brand new family, made up only of a husband and wife, certainly can live on less than after the children begin to come. Food and clothing expenses, as well as the possible need for a larger home or vehicle, will grow over time. As a result, a career does not have to start large, but a man will likely want to be in a profession that can grow with his expenses.

This growth could come in the form of climbing the corporate ladder, moving from employment to self-employment, or if they might be starting a business from the beginning, to grow that business over time. As we have said many times, it's not the purpose of this book to suggest what decision is right, only to encourage thorough discussion. Your sons will love you for the care and concern shown. There is plenty of joy just in the journey.

Another consideration is that as the leader of a home matures, he will need to be ready to assist others in need. A younger man still needs to be ready to give at a moment's notice. But a son should build into his long-term plans the ability to be in a position someday to truly help those in the Body as needs arise. And maybe even be able to help their sons establish themselves in a business.

**Can the skills and/or relationships involved in the profession be passed down to the next generation?**

When trying to help your sons choose careers, another thought to keep in mind is whether or not it involves an expertise that can be used to help *their* sons get started. If Dad has learned a special technique or specialized process that is in high demand, and parts of that knowledge are passed down to a son, the son will have a definite advantage over others that might apply for a particular job. Even those things that aren't highly specialized can still be caught just by being around a profession for a period of time, and provide an advantage over others hitting a field cold.

Also, in a profession that is relationship oriented, as most are, the father can really help his son succeed. Widget people tend to know other widget people, and if Dad enjoys a good reputation, the widget movers and shakers will want to do business with his son. Everyone agrees that who you know is more important than what you know, and if you can help your son, or if *your* son can pick a profession in which he can someday help *his* son, these are all good things.

## Could the skills and/or relationships be turned into a family business some day?

Isn't this every family's dream? To work alongside your family with common purpose seems to have universal appeal. But most families would have trouble pulling it off in this economy. Capital rules. Families that are struggling just to make ends meet will find it very difficult to save enough money to fund a small business startup.

So, if your son could use the relationships formed in his chosen career to later make it easier to spin something off, that would be wonderful. And at the very least, even if he didn't have the capital to start something with his own money, by being in a field where he is good at what he does and enjoys a good reputation, he might be able to attract investors.

## Is the profession noble and pure?

When deciding on a career path, above all else, the pursuit must be noble and pure. By noble, we mean the product or service is: 1) worthwhile, 2) needed, 3) good for the consumer, and 4) puts the seller and buyer on an even playing field. A gambling casino is not noble because it fails all four tests. Trying to sell unneeded products or services to the elderly or disadvantaged would also not be noble. Even some professions in the health and science fields may need to be considered carefully, as many schools and work environments do not have the respect we have for human life. These are tough issues, though, because reforming influences within those professions could have a lasting impact on our culture.

In addition, the purity factor is very important. The culture of some professions is, unfortunately, profane. Even though the work can be noble, the environment is rough. Some may avoid four years of college to escape the impurity of those surroundings, but then place themselves in a situation where, for forty years, they are around those who are crude and disrespectful of God's people and institutions, especially of the family. You certainly can help take back these vocations if you can contribute to the direction of the company through ownership or management, or work for a Christian company, but we wanted to issue a caution for your further reflection. Work in the trades has great potential, though, for starting a family business, and what a blessing that would be.

We hope these reflections have given you some things to think about, and will help you start with the end in mind. A little preparation and a lot of talking now, while your sons are still at home, could save them from wasted time and heartache later. We owe it to our sons to run out ahead using our experience and maturity to help guide and direct their paths.

We recently read a book by Steve Maxwell entitled *Preparing Sons to Provide for a Single Income Family.*[27] We also had the opportunity to hear him and his wife, Teri, speak at a conference. Steve certainly talks about the income side of the ledger, as we just discussed, but he really had some profound things to say about the expense side as well. He encouraged us to question two main areas as we raise our sons and daughters.

The first was his discussion of the "appetites" we give our children. If we belong to a country club, if we go on an extravagant vacation every year, or even if all we do is buy the best fishing equipment available, we are teaching them to have tastes they might not be able to afford when they establish their own homes. One of the reasons our generation has struggled so much with debt is that we expected to live as our parents did from the first day out on our own. We need to be careful of the lifestyle we are making normal for our children.

The other expense side issue is how much we teach them around the house. If they understand basic carpentry, plumbing, electrical, automotive, etc., our sons won't need to hire those services out when things break. And what son wouldn't want to work alongside his father to learn these things?

We would also like to take this concept and make another argument for our children not going away to college. Those four years could be spent working together and learning ever more complex skills around the house. And while at an age where they can really strengthen their abilities. If they were away, they might also lose opportunities to apprentice with a tradesman or help a widow around her house. These experiences will help shape the man, and to trade that for the companionship of fools doesn't seem to be very wise.

# CHAPTER 6

---

# PREPARING TO BE A
# WELL-EQUIPPED HELPMEET

We'd like to start by saying that we understand that this topic, the role of women in the home and in the workforce, can be a sensitive subject. And we certainly are not holding ourselves up as the authority here. We believe each father of a Christian home, with the counsel of his wife and the hearts of his daughters, should feel empowered to make good decisions for the future of his girls.

We pray that he takes this noble task seriously, though, because girls make themselves vulnerable by trusting in their father's leading. Men, we have to live up to their faith in us. We can't just sit back and hope something good happens in their lives, in their training, and in the choosing of a spouse. Instead, we must be proactive, and our prayers need to be way out ahead of theirs. We can't live our lives in a fog without a plan, and we also can't just follow the crowd and send them off to college, unprotected, for four years, just because everyone else does.

A good and right plan for your daughters may be no college at all, but even that shouldn't come without vision. Similarly, they shouldn't go away to school, or even college in town, until the desired end is clear. In all things, be a true leader, have a strategy, and commit to completing the work. They need that from you!

So, what are some of the principles involved in deciding on a course of action for our girls? We believe the biblical teachings, assuming she is not called to singleness, are as follows:

1) A woman is called to be a helper for her husband
2) A woman is called to be a keeper at home
3) A woman is called to raise and nurture children
4) A woman is to be known for her good deeds
5) A woman is called to be industrious and productive

### A woman is called to be a helper for her husband

As we all know, a woman's role as helper was not meant to give the husband permission to treat her disrespectfully, but to share a beautiful, abundant life together and multiply the work the man is able to accomplish. God told the man to be fruitful and multiply and have dominion over the earth and that dominion is bringing it under God's purposes. Therefore, having a helper in his wife, as they will also raise their children to be about the Lord's business, is a very good thing.

*Then the Lord God said, "It is not good that the man should be alone; I will make him a helper fit for him." (Genesis 2:18)*

We will talk more about Proverbs 31 later, but the first three verses of the excellent wife passage states:

*An excellent wife who can find? She is far more precious than jewels. The heart of her husband trusts in her, and he will have no lack of gain. She does him good, and not harm, all the days of her life. (Proverbs 31:10-12)*

These verses definitely presume her role as a contributor to her husband's vision and a key team member in the functioning of the family. Yes, she is working hard, but it is all under the headship and blessing of her husband. She cares about his reputation and she longs to bring him "good, and not harm, all the days of her life." His reputation is her crown.

As the excellent wife is described, when she engages in commerce, keeps her home, helps the poor, and is ready with wise instruction, she is blessing her husband, and he praises her. And through it all, "strength and dignity are her clothing" (v. 25). So, she is not timid or withdrawn, and has not lost her identity, but she understands that what she does is as helper to her husband's calling.

Again, from the nineteenth century book *Home-Making*, J.R. Miller states this concept very well, focusing not so much on what she does, but the heart of doing it:

> *Every true wife makes her husband's interests her own. While he lives for her, carrying her image in his heart and toiling for her all the days, she thinks only of what will do him good. When burdens press upon him she tries to lighten them by sympathy, by cheer, by the inspiration of love. She enters with zest and enthusiasm into all his plans. She is never a weight to drag him down; she is strength in his heart to help him ever to do nobler and better things.*[28]

How does all this apply to your daughter's education? The answer lies in how you can best equip her to be a qualified and effective helper for her future husband. You have the obligation, not just for her sake but for the sake of the Kingdom, to teach her well. If she is to help her husband with his mission, she needs to be capable of providing that help.

Depending on whom she marries, and what vocation he is led to, she will need to possess different skills. We have to leave most of the details to Providence, but there are some things to consider. We won't stress now that by being a keeper at home, nurturing children, doing good, and being industrious, she is most definitely being a helper in his vision. These are discussed next. But, the concept of how she can help with his profession, is worthy of some dialogue here.

We firmly believe that a father has the privilege to protect his daughter until she marries and comes under the love and protection of her husband. We also believe that before she marries, a father can be equipping his daughter to assist him in his business. In our family, in order to keep the bookstore running smoothly, it takes the time and talents of all our children. But we never could have done it without the wisdom and diligence of our oldest daughter, Katie. We are able to use her talents, while also keeping her protected, working alongside her family at our store. Even if these particular skills are never needed again, though, she has been learning the concept of serving others and learning basic business skills that will almost certainly be helpful later in life.

These concepts can apply even if the father works for someone else. The bookstore doesn't support our family, so I (Scott) have another full-time job. By our daughter focusing on the business of the store so much, she frees me to continue pursuing our main source of income. She and the other older children see their role in my full-time profession as encouragers, helping me sort papers, helping me pack for trips, and even coming to the office occasionally to help me with a big project or just to get organized. It's not so much what is done as it is the understanding of their calling as helpers.

If your daughter's future husband had a small business of his own or otherwise needed help in his work, the question becomes how best to prepare your daughter? Would some coursework after high school be helpful to this end? Is there any value in a degree or would it just be a waste of time and money? You're probably hoping we will answer these questions for you, but we're going to disappoint you. We really don't want to give such detailed advice, because we are very intent on sticking with the principle and not telling a family what is best for them. We hope we have given some helpful ideas to consider, though.

### A woman is called to be a keeper at home

The idea here is that no matter how busy a wife and mother becomes, it cannot be at the expense of keeping the home a lovely, sweet, orderly place of discipleship and ministry to her own family and hospitality to others. It is the base and refuge from a sometimes tough world and a spot where a family can dream and scheme of what they can do for their Lord. Again, in Deuteronomy 6, only the "walking by the way" is outside the home. The home is the principal place of training children and passing down the wonderful works of God.

And here, as in the previous section, it is a training ground for our girls as they see their mother live out these principles. A daughter should be helping her mother make their home this wonderful place. How domestic everyone becomes, how often the family eats out, whether the family makes their own clothes, or whether they bake their own bread, are all areas of preference and liberty, but a warm and sweet home should always be the standard. This takes time and energy, and a daughter should learn this art years before she ever has a home of her own.

Again, the question needs to be asked: What education should a girl receive to prepare her for being a keeper at home? Cooking classes, sewing classes, instruction on how to live on less? Probably most of these are best learned under the tutelage of her mother, but maybe a class or two would be fun. That's completely up to your family.

**A woman is called to raise and nurture children**

*But we were gentle among you, like a nursing mother taking care of her own children. (1 Thessalonians 2:7)*

A godly mother will gently care for her little ones. There will be discipline at times, and the setting of limits is incredibly important, but more than anything we want our daughters to learn to love with an undying love, and have great affection for, their children. What we are speaking of here is a tender, beautiful, and most of all joyful, relationship between mother and child that makes them feel warm, secure and cherished.

The gaining and keeping of their children's hearts will flow naturally as they feel their parents' abiding love. In this age of daycare, preschool, and mother's day out, the simple thought of "a mother taking care of her own children" is an extremely beautiful and refreshing thought. This biblical model is fundamental to finding family reformation. In Titus 2, Paul instructs the older women to teach the younger women to "love their husbands and children."

Another one of our favorite books, and probably our most loved on the subject of bringing up godly children, is Andrew Murray's book *Raising Your Children For Christ*. Andrew Murray was a very prolific writer in the late 1800s. He was a South African missionary and pastor, and because his flock was so large and so spread out, he decided the only way to really reach his people was to begin writing. In total, he wrote over 240 books. We would commend any of them to you.

Following are the concluding words of Reverend Murray's book:

> *Love that draws is more than love that demands. Training children requires a life of self-sacrifice. It requires love that 'seeketh not its own,' but lives and gives of itself. God has given the wonderful gift of mother-love. When this love is directed into the right channel, it becomes the handmaid of God's redeeming love. Rules and regulations presented without love always bring about sin and bitterness. Love gives itself, with all its thought and strength, to live for others. Love breathes its own stronger and better life into the weaker one. Love inspires, and this inspiration is the secret of training.*[29]

A child who understands that he has the unconditional love of his mother, and father too of course, will better understand God's love and will have the blessing of a "stronger and better life" breathed into him.

It's not just a mother's loving care that is needed, though; she is also called to teach. One of the requirements to be put on the widow's list in 1 Timothy 5 is that she has the reputation, and the fruit to show, that she has "brought up children." The first chapter of Proverbs also states that a mother's teaching will be "a graceful garland for your head and pendants for your neck."

So, what should we be teaching our daughters in order that they will be qualified to teach their children? Is there any formal education to help train them for this task? Unfortunately, we can't think of any place to get this training in a formal setting. Maybe that's not unfortunate, though, because it is undoubtedly better delivered in the context of the home and the church through the older women in their lives.

Speaking of older women, we pray your daughters enjoy the blessings of knowing many true "older women" as they are quite scarce in today's church. It seems as though travel, leisure, career, and a deafening inward focus are the hallmarks of this critical link in God's plan for helping raise our young ladies. Until the forty, fifty, sixty, seventy, eighty and ninety-somethings in the church wake up and understand the role they are created to play, the church will continue to struggle and our girls will continue to find their heroes in the culture. On the contrary, the woman described in Proverbs 31, obviously mature, "opens her mouth with wisdom, and the teaching of kindness is on her tongue."

**A woman is to be known for her good deeds**

More requirements for a woman to be placed on the widow's list are that she should have "a reputation for good works; if she has... shown hospitality, has washed the feet of the saints, has cared for the afflicted, and has devoted herself to every good work." Proverbs 31 also says, "She opens her hand to the poor and reaches out her hands to the needy." A real education involves all these things. Don't let your teaching stop at what is contained in textbooks, but give your girls, and your boys, the love of serving others when they are young. It will become normal for them, they will in turn delight in doing these things, and then when they are grown they will do them on their own initiative. Parents, isn't this is our goal? Don't settle for anything less!

And doesn't it start with us? Our children are not going to imitate what is not being modeled, so we as parents need to demonstrate this serving spirit. This is one of Andrew Murray's greatest theses in his book; the promise that our children will follow us, for good or for evil.

*It is this whole-hearted devotion that will give strength to our faith and confidence to our hope. Under its inspiration our prayers will be persevering and believing. It will impart to our instruction the joyful tone of assurance, and make our whole life the model for our children. It is one generation living for God that will secure the next for Him. I must expect that my whole-hearted consecration to God will guide them, because His salvation is from generation to generation.[30]*

Doing good for others does not come from a textbook, but from The Book, and the model of a surrendered life that serves Him always.

## A woman is called to be industrious and productive

As we alluded to before, a wife is meant to be strong. The excellent wife portrayed in Proverbs 31 is busy. She "does not eat the bread of idleness," but she is accomplishing things. She is helping the needy. She is serving her family. She is not a Victorian princess, meant only to be beheld. Of course she is the weaker vessel and husbands must be careful not to heap burdens upon her that she was not created to carry. In fact, a husband must carry *all* the burdens of the family, only delegating part of the load to his bride as she has time and is able. And of course she must be treated kindly, compassionately, tenderly and lovingly. But, at the same time, she also does not need to be treated as if she might break.

*She dresses herself with strength and makes her arms strong. (Proverbs 31:17)*

J.R. Miller writes:

*What is the ideal of a wife? It is not something lifted above the common experiences of life, not an ethereal angel feeding on ambrosia and moving in the realms of fancy... So there are ideals of womanhood which are lovely, full of graceful charms, pleasing, attractive, but which are too delicate and frail for this prosaic, storm-swept world of ours. Such ideals the poets and the novelists sometimes give us. They appear well to the eye as they are portrayed for us on the brilliant page. But of what use would they be in the life which the real woman of our day has to live? A breath of earthly air will stain them. One day of actual experience in the hard toils and sore struggles of life would shatter their frail loveliness to fragments. We had better seek for ideals which will not be soiled by a rude touch nor blown away by a stiff breeze, and which will grow lovelier as they move through life's paths of sacrifice and toil. The true wife needs to be no mere poet's dream, no artist's picture, no ethereal lady too little for use, but a woman healthful, strong, practical, industrious, with a hand for life's common duties, yet crowned with that beauty which a high and noble purpose gives to a soul.[31]*

### ANY ROLE FOR HIGHER EDUCATION?

Now, how does college fit in, or not fit in? Our personal philosophy is that there should not be an artificial barrier put up between twelfth grade and college-level courses, especially knowing that there are ways to achieve college credit while still in high school and often without compromise beyond that. We would never put our girls at risk for the sake of college, but if taking more courses has the potential of equipping them to be better wives and mothers, we believe that can be a wise choice.

On the other side of that argument, college could provide the potential to meet ungodly peers and could end up being a trap and a snare for our girls. There is also the consideration of giving them appetites for more worldly pursuits and a career orientation. Again, these decisions are up to the family, but we think a caution is warranted.

What are the different paths a girl could take? We encourage you to sit down with your daughters and think through what skills might be helpful, other than those better taught by her parents and elders in her life. Kris has been a great blessing to our family with the medical knowledge she has been able to accumulate over the years. She began with some formal medical education when she was college age and then has learned most of the rest on her own as the mother of eight children.

As a result, our oldest daughter, Katie, has had a personal interest in medicine as well and has continued some medical-related coursework. She hopes to become a better medical consumer for her family and to be a blessing to others. We think the idea here is to concentrate on what "education" might be helpful and not what "career" to pursue.

One more thought to consider would be that we never know what circumstances may befall our girls where having some additional preparation would be a blessing. The first part of another of Cotton Mather's Resolutions, states:

> *Among all the points of education which I will endeavor for my children, I hope to see that each of them — the daughters as well as the sons — may gain insight into some skill that lies in the way of gain (however their own inclination may most carry them), so that they may be able to subsist themselves, and get something of a livelihood, in case the Providence of God should bring them into necessities.*[32]

So, even in the days of the Puritans it was considered prudent, at least by Cotton Mather, to give all his children, "the daughters as well as the sons... some skill that lies in the way of gain." This does not necessarily mean college, as there are many skills a young lady could attain where she might be able to make a living apart from a formal degree "in case the Providence of God should bring [her] into necessities," but we believe this thought is something to throw in the mix.

A very important point to be made, though, is that it is always the role of the family, and then of the church, to take care of the fatherless and widows. But in today's weakened church, who knows what provision there will be for our daughters if they fail them. It may be sensible to follow Mather's advice and be thinking of whether or not the teaching of such a skill, or at least the plan for learning one quickly, should be part of her training.

# SECTION III

---

# PRACTICAL CONSIDERATIONS

# CHAPTER 7

---

# COST OF COLLEGE,
# STEWARDSHIP & DEBT

Everyone knows about the cost of higher education. Wow, what a burden to place on either the parents of a child or on the child himself. The College Board, in their Annual Survey of Colleges, shows 2003-04 costs per resident student, including all fees, housing, books and supplies, to be $29,541 for private institutions, $13,833 for in-state public higher education and $20,879 for out-of-state public institutions.[33] In addition, costs have been going up in excess of eight percent per year over the last ten years.[34] Even if we assume a constant increase of just six percent, a child entering college in 2005 will be spending, over the next four years, $145,000 for a private school, $68,000 for in-state public, and $103,000 for out-of-state public.

How do parents save that much money for one child, let alone multiple children? Especially since we homeschoolers tend to have more than the national average of 2.2 children, is paying for traditional college even feasible? And even if your family has the means, is it good stewardship?

A dollar that your family earns can only be used once, and it is exciting to consider what other good could come from those resources if not spent on college. How about down payments on homes for your children? How about retiring some debt? How about helping families in need? How about just sending a check to a young, struggling family in your church? What about helping a single mother on a monthly basis so she can stay at home and homeschool her children? What about helping a family adopt?

> *Religion that is pure and undefiled before God, the Father, is this: to visit orphans and widows in their affliction, and to keep oneself unstained from the world. (James 1:27)*

This verse not only tells us that taking care of those in affliction, specifically orphans and widows, is very pleasing to Him, it also mentions that we should keep ourselves from being stained by the world. With a traditional college, we have a choice of whether to put our children at risk of being stained, or save that money and potentially do some great things for the Kingdom. Something to seriously consider!

Don't forget, however, that we are not talking about whether to get a college degree or not, but whether to take the "traditional" path or not. The independent study approach, through the fully accredited colleges to be highlighted later, can produce a full bachelor's degree for about $6,000. If college is something you believe is in God's will for some of your children, this is the approach, or some sensible combination of independent and traditional, that we are encouraging.

So, if it doesn't make sense for the parents to pay, what about the child paying? There certainly are scholarships, grants and student loans to help fund part of the initial expense. But, unfortunately, scholarships and grants don't normally pay for a particularly large share of the expense, if a student qualifies at all, and loans must be paid back. The average amount of an individual grant in 2002-03, taken from the College Board study mentioned above, is $7,300 at private schools and $2,400 at public colleges and universities.[35] About half of all undergraduate students receive some form of grant.[36]

As far as student loans are concerned, they are obviously a very popular option for today's student. However, the average student loan debt at the end of an undergraduate college career, according to a 2002 study by Nellie Mae, was $21,200 for those attending private institutions, $17,100 for publics, and combining for an overall average of $18,900.[37] Assuming the $18,900 loan balance above, the 2004-05 Federal Stafford Loan variable repayment interest rate of 3.37 percent, and considering the maximum repayment term of 10 years, monthly payments beginning six months after graduation would be $185 per month.[38] If a young man would begin his career today with a $30,000 salary, $185 a month is about 11 percent of a 70 percent take-home pay.

The table on the following page illustrates the challenge that college expenses can be and the burden it places on the young person who must fund most of its costs through loans:

## Example of Total College Costs and Funding Sources
Assumes Student Has $30,000 of Cash and/or Wages From Work While in College
Four-Year Average Projected Costs for Student Beginning 2005-06 Term
Includes Tuition & Fees, Room & Board, Books & Supplies, Transportation and Other Costs

| | Private College | In-State Public | Out-of-State Public |
|---|---|---|---|
| **Expenses** | | | |
| 4-Year Average Total Cost (1) | $145,000 | $68,000 | $103,000 |
| Average Grants (2) | 34,000 | 11,000 | 11,000 |
| Net Cost After Grants | $111,000 | $57,000 | $92,000 |
| **Funding Sources** | | | |
| Student Cash and/or Work Proceeds (3) | $30,000 | $30,000 | $30,000 |
| Maximum Stafford Loan (4) | 23,000 | 23,000 | 23,000 |
| Remainder from Nellie Mae EXCEL Loan | 58,000 | 4,000 | 39,000 |
| Total Cash Funding | $111,000 | $57,000 | $92,000 |
| **Loan Expenses Added to Original Loan Amounts** | | | |
| Stafford Loan Fees & Deferred Interest (5) | $3,576 | $3,576 | $3,576 |
| Stafford Loan Balance at Graduation | 26,576 | 26,576 | 26,576 |
| EXCEL Loan Fees & Deferred Interest (6) | 18,478 | 1,274 | 12,425 |
| EXCEL Loan Balance at Graduation | 76,478 | 5,274 | 51,425 |
| **Monthly Payments at Graduation (10 Year Term)** | | | |
| Stafford Monthly Payment (7) | $260 | $260 | $260 |
| EXCEL Monthly Payment (8) | 873 | 60 | 587 |
| Total Monthly Payment | $1,134 | $321 | $848 |
| **Loan Payments as Percentage of Take-Home Pay** | | | |
| Projected Starting Salary in 2009 | $40,000 | $40,000 | $40,000 |
| Projected Take-Home Pay (70%) | 28,000 | 28,000 | 28,000 |
| 12 Total Monthly Payments | 13,604 | 3,848 | 10,172 |
| Percentage of Take-Home Pay | 49% | 14% | 36% |

NOTES:

(1)    Derived from 2003-04 College Board study and inflated for student beginning 2005-06
(2)    Derived from 2002-03 Nellie Mae study and inflated for student beginning 2005-06
(3)    Assumes combination of savings, gifts and/or wages from work while in college totaling $30,000
(4)    Maximum for student still dependent of parents (maximum is $46,000 if independent)
(5)    Up to 4% fee plus 2004-05 annual interest of 2.77% while in school (variable rate at 91-day T-bill + 1.70%)
(6)    2% fee if using co-borrower and 2004-05 annual interest charges of 6.75% (variable rate at prime + 2.25%)
(7)    2004-05 interest rate of 3.37% (variable rate at 91-day T-bill + 2.30%)
(8)    2004-05 interest rate of 6.75% does not change after graduation

This illustration assumes a student would already have $30,000 through savings, gifts from relatives, or would be able to raise that amount working his way through school (possibly in another impure environment). The rest would be through student loans. Given this example, a new graduate in 2009 would expect to spend 49 percent of his take-home pay on student loan payments if he attended the average private school, 14 percent for an in-state public and 36 percent for an out-of-state public. This is an incredible burden on a person trying to establish a new home of his own. If a student was eligible for an above-average scholarship or would have other funding sources, these numbers could change dramatically, but this example is based on the national average costs and assuming, again, $30,000 of personal cash.

If your vision is that your grandchildren will not be in daycare, you must plan for it now. We know of families who would have loved to start their family right away and be able to afford for the wife to stay at home, but a debt burden created by two students marrying, after both paying for college through loans, made it very difficult. Take the above example and multiply the expense times two, leaving the income the same. Where does that get you? It makes it very hard to find more money than there is month, not to mention the stress on a new marriage. Vision now will pay huge dividends later!

The stewardship argument also comes into play with the loan approach. Even if a student thought he could afford the payments, is committing yourself to this much debt a good idea? How many Kingdom-building opportunities would you miss? How much more would you be enslaved to your employer? How many opportunities to start a family business would be passed over because of the debt burden?

In case we are putting a serious guilt trip on anyone who believes God may be calling them to a traditional college, we must restate that our objective is not to make decisions for other families, only to warn of the potential pitfalls. Also, the independent study approach does have some limitations on the number of available majors. Degrees requiring clinicals, degrees with very specialized coursework, and some other professional degrees can be tough to pull off using this method for the entire course of study. However, always remember that even if you can't get the entire degree with this approach, you can always use a hybrid and complete as many courses as possible independently. Potentially, you could be required only to take your upper level courses at a traditional college. And staying in town is almost always the better choice, both from a cost and a spiritual viewpoint.

We have a good friend who is working on a degree in actuarial science. This degree is not offered by the independent study schools, but is obtainable from a university in town. He took many of his initial courses through the independent study approach and was able to transfer them without a problem.

Since I (Scott) am in the insurance business, I know that the actuarial field is a very good one. It pays well enough to support a large family, and it creates the potential for working at home some day. My fourteen-year-old son has also considered this as a potential career, and since I am in the industry, though I am not an actuary myself, I might be able to help him get established through my contacts.

The actuarial degree, because it is a very specialized major, is only available at a few institutions. So, this would mean that a student would need to adopt a combined or blended approach. Many, many of the credits can be attained using the alternative method, leaving far fewer credits to be taken at the university, and thereby saving a boatload. Instead of $6,000, this degree may end up costing more like $30,000 to $40,000, but they should still be able to finish quite early and the extra investment may be worth it for the other benefits this degree offers.

The message we are trying to convey is that for every young person there are different circumstances, different dreams, different interests, different talents, and different economic constraints. Using these concepts, however, we hope we have given you some things to consider to make the degree as inexpensive as possible, showing good stewardship, without debt, and avoiding most of the compromising situations so prevalent in today's higher education environment.

# CHAPTER 8

---

## INEFFICIENCY OF
## CLASSROOM LEARNING

Just as a traditional college is often a poor use of your money, traditional college courses can also be a poor use of your child's time. As a homeschooler, you have become accustomed to the tutor, or independent study, approach where when your student masters the material, you move on. Our two oldest children have taken dual enrollment classes at a local college, and their first day of class there was their first day of class ever. One of the earliest comments about their experience was how slowly the professor covered the material. If they were on their own, they could have finished the coursework in just a few weeks, but with having to wait on the professor and the rest of the class, they took the whole sixteen-week semester.

It is our experience and counsel that classroom learning is very inefficient. Just think back to your high school or college days and remember all the extra things you had to do that had very little bearing on the subject at hand. In our daughter's microbiology class, the first two-hour lab was only about how to use a microscope. Then, in the second lab, it was about the same thing! A lot more could have been accomplished in those four hours.

In addition to Cotton Mather's Resolutions quoted already, Jonathan Edwards wrote some of his own. His fifth Resolution, written around 1720, states:

*Resolved, never to lose one moment of time; but improve it the most profitable way I possibly can.*[39]

One of our observations of the American church is the incredible amount of time wasted. We are caught up as much in the "need" for rest and relaxation as the world is. This should not be. Diligent work is a biblical virtue and should not be overlooked.

*In all toil there is profit, but mere talk tends only to poverty.*
*(Proverbs 14:23)*

*Let the favor of the Lord our God be upon us, and establish the work of our hands upon us; yes, establish the work of our hands!*
*(Psalm 90:17)*

So, stay diligent and consider the idea of finishing quickly. Why not let your children get on with their adult lives? Why not prepare them for marriage early? With this approach there is no reason they can't finish a degree in a year or two. Certainly, your circumstances may be very different, but with getting a good number of credits out of the way before college age, this timeframe should work.

Our culture embraces a prolonged adolescence that often extends well into a person's twenties. We believe, and history bears this out, that we expect way too little of our young people. They can be much more productive than we give them credit for, and they would be much happier making a contribution to the family, to the church, and to their future by getting on with their adult life. Jonathan Edwards, for example, entered Yale at the age of thirteen and was pastoring a church by nineteen.[40]

What could the church's next generation accomplish if we just expected more of them? They won't break, and they won't rebel. To the contrary, they will love you for it as long as you also pump the vision. Let them see why they work hard. What is the goal? What is the prize? Show them the finish line, and help show them the path.

*The simple believes everything, but the prudent gives thought to his steps. (Proverbs 14:15)*

There are also other reasons that the independent study model is more efficient. Not only can you knock out college credits more quickly and get on with your life, you can also be prudent about which subjects you learn more thoroughly, thereby spending more time on the course material you want to keep with you in adulthood and move quickly through the material you would just as soon forget.

Take Psychology, for example, which is a required course for many majors. There are a number of reasons to take a CLEP test on a course like this:

1) Just studying a CLEP course guide for this subject might only take a couple weeks to immerse yourself in the topic and prepare for the test, thereby saving fourteen weeks of a sixteen-week traditional course.

2) Cramming in the material on a course like this, in our opinion, is a *good* idea because there is not much worthwhile to keep in your long-term memory from a secular psychology curriculum.

3) It avoids all the "group learning" (yikes!) in a regular college class. Who knows where some of those conversations may go? Only one kid does the work anyway and the rest sponge off of them.

4) It circumvents a long research paper on some bizarre behavior better explained by the Scriptures than by Sigmund Freud.

5) You can *purposefully* attempt to barely get a passing grade and avoid learning too much.

6) You can stay more involved with the regular family schedule by not being tied to a class schedule and whatever group activities might be required.

While we were having some fun with this, there is a lot of truth in the above. Some classes required for particular degrees will be questionable at best. So, while the course may be required, it would not be a fruitful use of time to learn it well. As stated before, the independent study approach allows you to spend more time on the good courses and much less on the ones that are problematic or just plain dumb.

And it's not just courses in classrooms that can be inefficient. Our friend, Nathanael Cordz, whose course of study is detailed in Chapter 15, had to take one online course for his business degree. The rest of his degree was all independent study, but Thomas Edison State College required him to take this one course. Even though it was over the internet, it was not self-paced, so he had to wait for new assignments from the professor. It still took sixteen weeks. So, not all distance learning is independent. Much of it works like a classroom course without the desks and chairs, and it still costs about as much as a class in a physical location.

# CHAPTER 9

---

## MORE FOCUSED
## TRAINING

Most higher education institutions require a great deal of liberal arts and general education courses that may or may not contribute to the learning that will be used in a particular field. We definitely believe in a good, well-rounded education, but some of the courses should just as soon be glossed over or skipped completely.

The independent study institutions allow you to tailor, to a large extent, your own curriculum within reasonably-established parameters. The insurance industry, as an example, offers many courses that lead to professional designations that can enhance your career. The independent study colleges will grant credit for these professional courses, giving a person a real head start toward establishing himself in his field.

And these courses provide some other benefits, also.

1) They are already designed for independent study, so they fit great into this approach.

2) They provide very valuable, specific pieces of information directly tailored to a particular field. With most college majors, a traditional bachelor's degree gives you the theory, and then working on the job gives you the practical application. These courses, because they are designed as continuing education for someone already in the field, tend to be much more practical and focused on knowledge you can use right away.

3) Most tests can be taken with very short notice, not just at designated times during the year.

4) They are reasonably priced. While they are more than a CLEP book and test, they are much less than a traditional college course. The most popular insurance designation is the Chartered Property Casualty Underwriter (CPCU) and each of its courses gives a student three hours of college credit under this approach for only about $350. This includes the books and the test fee.

We will be going into this topic in more detail in Chapter 14, *A Few More Tools*, but for now we wanted to at least introduce the topic in this chapter dealing with how the independent study approach can give you the flexibility to be so much more focused and deliberate.

And it is not just more focused with regard to your major, but you can also decide to take many of your electives in topics that are of interest to you or where you want to devote much of your time. Theology, music, art, history, language, nutrition, or agriculture, as examples, are areas where you may desire to develop proficiency just because you have an interest. The independent study approach will give you much more flexibility to bring your other interests into your curriculum and receive college credit in the process.

# CHAPTER 10

---

# POST-GRADUATE
# WORK

Our seventeen-year-old son, Steve, is seriously considering law as a vocation, and the independent study approach works wonderfully for those desiring post-graduate parchment. You can work to get your undergraduate degree out of the way quickly, and then focus your greater attention on the higher degree.

That graduate degree could come from a local class-based program or from one of a growing number of institutions offering master's programs via distance learning. Both of these options can still be expensive, but having the plan of getting a bachelor's degree from an independent study school and then getting started on a masters early, gives us some interesting points to consider:

1) Because the bachelor's degree is done very inexpensively, the master's degree may be easier to afford.

2) By starting in high school and moving quickly through a student's undergraduate studies, it is possible to finish a masters before peers are finished with a four-year degree.

3) Having a masters does give a person an edge in the marketplace. On average, people with master's degrees earn 19 percent more than those with just an undergraduate degree. And, by the way, people with a bachelors earn 72 percent more than those with only a high school education,

and these gaps have been widening steadily since the early 1980s.[41]

4) If a parent or student had any concerns about how a degree from one of the independent study schools would be perceived, those schools being Thomas Edison State College (New Jersey), Charter Oak State College (Connecticut), or Excelsior College (New York), a master's degree from a more well-known school would completely nullify any misperceptions by a potential employer. Now, that being said, we don't personally have concerns about degrees from these institutions because they are fully accredited, and a student can demonstrate a remarkable track record of being able to work hard, smart, creatively and independently.

5) A very large percentage of independent study institution graduates go on to get master's degrees. We have seen statistics that well over half of their graduates are accepted into graduate programs, and by some of the top schools, and in many different programs including law, medicine, divinity and business.

6) Other students in a master's program are typically older and less foolish than the typical college student, so the likelihood of bad influences in a classroom setting goes way down.

7) Many schools offer distance learning for their master's programs, so a student should be able to continue at home all the way through. Again, they are not necessarily less expensive, but it can be done without the distractions and wasted time of a classroom environment.

Now, back to my son's potential law aspirations. There is a very well respected independent study institution in California that grants law degrees. It is called Oak Brook College of Law and Government Policy, and reading part of their mission statement will tell you a lot about what they stand for.

80

*Oak Brook College approaches law and government policy from a Biblical and historical perspective. Oak Brook College students are committed to the self-evident truths articulated by our Founding Fathers in the Declaration of Independence and they reject the faith of evolution and the religion of secular humanism. Students learn the Biblical foundations of the Common Law and are challenged to make conventional application of these principles to resolve today's legal and governmental issues. Oak Brook College trains its students by using innovative distance-learning techniques, seminars, workshops and on-line instruction.*[42]

This institution loves homeschoolers, and we personally know several that have been trained, or are currently being trained, by the school. Admission requirements include either 60 hours of college credit or, in the alternative, only three CLEP tests. An entering student must also have attended a class-based Basic Life Principles Seminar.

Their law degree takes four years, tuition is currently $3,000 per year, and other fees over the four years are only about $1,800. A student must enter in August, and it begins with an on-site, one-week orientation and their Introduction to Law course. The rest of the coursework is all distance learning except for a seminar at the end of the first year to prepare for the First-Year Law Students' Examination. We have heard that this test is very difficult, and it is taken in California.

The main downside to this program is that while Oak Brook has been granted approval for their juris doctor degree in California, and graduates are eligible to take the California Bar Examination and be licensed to practice in that state, currently only four other states will allow graduates to sit for their respective state's bar. The reason is that the degree is non-accredited and the 45 states not allowing it require an accredited degree in addition to the passing of the Bar. There is an effort, however, to ask states to require only the passing of a Bar in another state for those licensed attorneys to sit for that state's exam. We'll all have to stay tuned.

What about medical school? Can we train our sons to be doctors using this method and without incurring tens of thousands of dollars of debt? We have heard stories of new doctors owing well over $100,000 in student loans using the traditional approach.

We have not done a great deal of research on this topic, but we can tell you that a bachelor's degree from one of the independent study schools is normally acceptable and, based on a conversation we had with a physician recently, can be part of an interesting history to help an application stand out with a medical school admissions committee. However, one of our local medical schools requires that some of the courses taken during the bachelor's degree need to be in a classroom at a traditional four-year college. They especially guard their science courses. So, if one of your students is considering medicine as a career, the best thing to do is ask a lot of questions of the medical school admissions department to get their advice. Everything we have heard is favorable for homeschoolers and for a non-traditional bachelor's degree, so don't be afraid if you believe this may be your child's calling. The world certainly needs godly physicians.

Now, as with the other post-graduate programs above, we don't know of a way to do medical school itself inexpensively, but if the bachelors is less expensive, it will cut down the overall cost quite dramatically. Also, we have heard of programs that will pay for part of medical school tuition in exchange for a prescribed number of years service in a rural area or in the military. So, ask around and be creative. Early planning would help immensely.

Finally, can seminary be done independently? We are pleased to say that dozens of seminaries will grant master's degrees almost totally through distance learning, and some take this approach all the way. One in particular that we are familiar with, Whitefield Theological Seminary, is all independent study with a mentoring approach, simply utilizing lecture tapes, a reading schedule and the assignment of papers.

Our loving God just keeps opening doors!

# SECTION IV

---

# WHAT ARE THE TOOLS?

# CHAPTER 11

---

# CREDIT BY
# EXAMINATION

Well, we're finally ready to explain how to do this. How do we go about getting a $6,000 college degree? And you say my child can start while he is still in high school and easily be done by his twentieth birthday? The answer is yes, and here's how it works.

The five tools we will discuss over the next several chapters include:

1) Credit by Examination
2) Dual Enrollment
3) Professional, Continuing Education
4) Distance Learning
5) Portfolio Assessment

Creatively combining these approaches under the guidelines of an independent study institution, described later in Chapter 15, can give your children that elusive college degree while staying at home, and at a price most of us have the means to scrape together. Or, as we stated previously, this approach can be utilized early and then blended with a traditional approach later.

With that very brief introduction to the tools, we are now ready to talk about the first, and probably most important, source of college credit. The overall category is termed "Credit By Examination" and includes plenty of acronyms like CLEP, DSST, ECE, TECEP and AP. These are the different types of tests. We will add one more acronym, though, to make the discussion a little easier. To refer to all the tests together, we will use "CBE" for Credit By Examination. The idea is that you can earn college credit for knowledge you have already acquired. You could have gained that knowledge through either formal or informal learning, but regardless, you are going to forego a class and simply take a test to earn the credit.

In the next chapter we will be describing the different methods of preparation, but for now we will turn to a description of each type of CBE. Please don't be discouraged as you read this section, though, as the amount of material may seem overwhelming. Please stick with us, and we think it will all come together in the end. If not, a rereading of this chapter later on may be helpful.

Given that disclaimer, the organizations offering CBE's include:
1) College Level Examination Program (CLEP)
2) DANTES Subject Standardized Tests (DSST)
3) Thomas Edison College Examination Program (TECEP)
4) Excelsior College Examinations (ECE)
5) Advanced Placement (AP)

## COLLEGE LEVEL EXAMINATION PROGRAM (CLEP)
### www.collegeboard.com

CLEP tests are by far the most popular CBE and ones that you may have heard of before. Most people begin with CLEP because the process is fairly easy to understand, the tests are convenient to take, the results are immediate, and the tests are primarily designed to cover the first two years of college requirements. Our first three children started with CLEP, and their experiences were all positive.

These tests are administered by the College Board, which is a non-profit organization that also offers the SAT, PSAT/NMSQT, and AP programs. CLEP tests are ninety minutes in length and are five-choice multiple choice, with the exception of English Composition, which can include an optional essay. They are graded instantly by the computer, so you know before you leave the testing center whether you passed or not (again with the exception of the English Comp essay). CLEP's are accepted by nearly three thousand higher education institutions around the country, and the test centers are located in over thirteen hundred of those. However, some of the testing sites will allow only their own enrolled students to sit for the exams. A full list of sites, and whether they are open to the public, can be found on the College Board website listed above.

Living in metropolitan St. Louis, there are three testing centers within fifteen minutes of our home. You may want to look at each of the sites close to you, because each of the three near us offers a fairly different environment. Our favorite one is at Maryville University, because you get to take the tests in a quiet, private room. The staff is also very helpful, friendly and enjoys homeschoolers. Another of the sites close to us is altogether different. Students sit in an open room with rows of computers, and are there taking several different types of tests of varying lengths. Although we also find this college to be very homeschool friendly, we have found the environment to be distracting, especially for a younger student. Our third option close to us falls between the two.

There are no age restrictions on taking a CLEP, but they will be looking for identification. We have used driver's licenses, driver's permits, and for Joe, our youngest test taker at age thirteen, we used a passport that was made when he was nine. That was pretty funny!

If your child is under sixteen with no passport, you may want to call the testing center in advance and find out what they accept. We understand that identification cards might be available from a state's license offices. Regardless, we figure they won't question the younger kids too much, because after all, who would want to cheat by sending in a thirteen year old to take a college level test for them!

Another great thing about CLEP is that you do not have to be enrolled in college to begin taking the exams. Included in the fee is the cost of holding, or banking, your credits at the CLEP Center for up to twenty years, so you can have them transferred to the institution of your choice at any time. At the beginning of the exam, you will be asked to pick an institution that you want the results sent to, but we suggest you choose not to send them anywhere. That way your results will only go to CLEP and be stored there for later use.

The reason you should bank them instead of sending them directly to a college is twofold: 1) in case your child does not pass, it doesn't go on a college transcript, so no one will ever know, and 2) he probably doesn't know yet where he will enroll, or he might change his mind later.

If your child's plan is to use CLEP exams as a start and later graduate from a traditional college, we recommend making a short list of the potential schools you may be considering. Each school has an established policy for which CLEP's they accept for credit. This list may be in their handbook, on the internet, or you may need to call their admissions department. If you are going to call, ask for an advisor familiar with the requirements for transfer students. The general admissions advisors, who are often students working part time, are usually not familiar with how credits are transferred and what is acceptable.

Be assured that CLEP credits are easily transferred to the vast majority of universities. However, most have limits on the number of CLEP credit hours that can count toward a degree – thirty to sixty hours is average. Only the most selective schools refuse to accept any, although we have been told by a former admissions employee at a top school that they still look good on an application, demonstrating initiative and the ability to master college-level work.

Remember that these restrictions only apply to traditional schools, so they are applicable only if you plan to use the blended approach. The independent study colleges in Chapter 15 don't limit you, but if your desire is to finish at a regular school, you need to make sure you know the rules before charging ahead too strongly.

Also, for the blended approach, there are still a few traditional colleges that will charge you their regular credit hour tuition to transfer in your CLEP work. Others will charge their dual enrollment rate. This is another good question to ask the admissions department before you get too far. Many charge only a nominal amount, but you may want to consider a different institution if they charge heavily for CLEP transfers.

But all that being said, CLEP's can become your best friend. They will allow you to take most of your first two years of credits for just $70 per test ($55 to CLEP and around $15 to the test site). This pays for either a three- or six-hour test. What an incredible value!

Also, CLEP's are great because you can take them whenever you are ready. You don't have to wait for a particular time of year or even time of day. Our favorite site offers them five days a week at 9:00, 11:00 and 1:00. You just call up the testing site, usually a couple days in advance, and make an appointment. Everything is at your pace, and you don't have to waste time waiting for the next testing opportunity.

CLEP tests are pass/fail, and there is no real penalty for failing. When you are ready to transfer your results to a college, you only call out the test dates where you passed. The only consequence of not passing is that you have to wait six months before you can take that test again. If you are in a hurry, that will hurt, but at least it doesn't technically count against you. This gives you the ability to even try a test with some of your middle school children just for fun, and to experiment with their ability to master some of these subjects. With the younger children, if they pass, you can decide to continue with more vigor. If they don't, you can wait a year or two and let them try again.

Below is a list of CLEP tests offered by the College Board, along with both military and general public pass rates. It also shows the credit hours recommended by the American Council on Education (ACE), which evaluates exams for the benefit of the higher education community. The ACE recommendations give colleges and universities a guideline for credit issuance. They are not binding, but most colleges follow their advice.

| CLEP<br>Test Title | Credit<br>Hours | Credit<br>Level | Military<br>Personnel<br>Pass<br>Rate | General<br>Public<br>Pass<br>Rate |
|---|---|---|---|---|
| **General:** | | | | |
| College Mathematics | 6 | L | 73% | 66% |
| English Composition (w/essay) | 6 | L | 68% | 53% |
| Humanities | 6 | L | 50% | - |
| Natural Sciences | 6 | L | 68% | 39% |
| Social Sciences & History | 6 | L | 67% | 49% |
| | | | | |
| **History & Social Sciences:** | | | | |
| American Government | 3 | L | 8% | 31% |
| Human Growth & Development | 3 | L | 33% | - |
| History of the US I | 3 | L | 53% | 83% |
| History of the US II | 3 | L | 44% | 67% |
| Introduction to Educational Psychology | 3 | L | 50% | - |
| Introductory Psychology | 3 | L | 53% | 88% |
| Introductory Sociology | 3 | L | 54% | - |
| Macroeconomics | 3 | L | 51% | 77% |
| Microeconomics | 3 | L | 41% | 76% |
| Western Civilization I | 3 | L | 48% | - |
| Western Civilization II | 3 | L | 42% | - |
| | | | | |
| **Composition & Literature:** | | | | |
| American Literature | 6 | L | 21% | 47% |
| Analyzing & Interpreting Literature | 6 | L | 58% | 77% |
| English Literature | 6 | L | 15% | 44% |
| Freshman College Composition | 6 | L | 76% | 94% |
| | | | | |
| **Science & Mathematics:** | | | | |
| Calculus with Elementary Functions | 6 | L | 28% | - |
| College Algebra | 3 | L | 25% | 61% |
| College Algebra/Trigonometry | 3 | L | 27% | - |
| General Biology | 6 | L | 26% | - |
| General Chemistry | 6 | L | 7% | - |
| Trigonometry | 3 | L | 39% | - |
| | | | | |
| **Business:** | | | | |
| Introductory Accounting | 6 | L | 26% | 56% |
| Introductory Business Law | 3 | L | 11% | - |
| Information Systems/Computers | 3 | L | 68% | - |
| Principles of Management | 3 | L | 60% | 89% |
| Principles of Marketing | 3 | L | 46% | - |
| | | | | |
| **Foreign Language:** | | | | |
| College French I | 6 | L | 63% | - |
| College French II | 12 | L | 63% | - |
| College German I | 6 | L | 85% | - |
| College German II | 12 | L | 85% | - |
| College Spanish I | 6 | L | 92% | - |
| College Spanish II | 12 | L | 92% | - |

Military pass rates are taken from an old DANTES website, no longer available
General public pass rates were provided by Maryville University in St. Louis

L = lower level course (freshman & sophomore)
U = upper level course (junior & senior)

The pass rates give your child an idea of how hard to study for a particular test. It also gives you a feel for which tests might be better for your younger children to start with, giving them a more confident start. For instance, our oldest three children started with the test History of the U.S. I, because it has one of the highest pass rates in its category, and history is almost always required for a bachelor's degree. Looking at the difference in pass rates between History of the U.S. I and American Government, the choice seems clear for your younger student who may just be getting his CLEP feet wet.

## DANTES SUBJECT STANDARDIZED TESTS (DSST)
### www.getcollegecredit.com

The DANTES exams were originally developed for military personnel, but they are now available to civilians as well. These tests are four-choice multiple choice. There is no time limit on the DSST's, as opposed to the ninety-minute limit on the CLEP's. However, everyone that we know who has taken one has finished in about ninety minutes anyway.

These tests are accepted at over nineteen hundred colleges and universities and are available at approximately six hundred testing centers. The testing centers are located on military bases and on many of the college campuses that also accept the tests. A state-by-state listing of test centers is on the website under the Colleges & Universities section. In some cases a school will only administer the tests for their enrolled students, but many are open to the general public. We have two sites very close to our home, and both are quite homeschool friendly. One of them is especially captivated by the homeschoolers that come in.

Of the total cost, $60 goes to DSST, and around $20 goes to the testing site. And as with the CLEP tests, you must wait six months before retaking a failed test.

Finally, DSST's are done on paper (the old #2 pencil type), and they do not offer instant results. They allow themselves four weeks to mail the results, but they usually come in two or three.

The website also has a great deal of information regarding the program, and there is a Fact Sheet available for each test that gives an overview of what the test will cover, some sample questions, the passing grade they recommend to colleges, and suggested textbooks to study. The website also offers study courses (online, CD, or printed workbook) and a printed study guide that covers eight of the most popular tests in one publication.

Their full study courses start at $129, plus books, and are currently available for twenty of the exams. The study guide covering the eight tests is only $15.96. The website also offers online practice tests for $4.95 each.

On the next page is the full DSST test list:

| DSST<br>Test Title | Credit<br>Hours | Credit<br>Level | Course<br>Available | Covered<br>in<br>Study<br>Guide | Military<br>Personnel<br>Pass<br>Rate |
|---|---|---|---|---|---|
| **Mathematics:** | | | | | |
| Fundamentals of College Algebra | 3 | L | Y | - | 26% |
| Principles of Statistics | 3 | L | Y | - | 37% |
| | | | | | |
| **Social Science:** | | | | | |
| Art of the Western World | 3 | L | - | - | 39% |
| Western Europe Since 1945 | 3 | L | - | - | 36% |
| An Introduction to Modern Middle East | 3 | L | - | - | 54% |
| Human/Cultural Geography | 3 | L | - | - | 56% |
| Rise & Fall of the Soviet Union | 3 | L/U | - | - | 47% |
| A History of the Vietnam War | 3 | L | - | - | 34% |
| The Civil War & Reconstruction | 3 | L/U | Y | - | 47% |
| Foundations of Education | 3 | L | - | - | 60% |
| Lifespan Developmental Psychology | 3 | L | Y | - | 44% |
| General Anthropology | 3 | L | - | - | 37% |
| Drug & Alcohol Abuse | 3 | L/U | Y | - | 40% |
| Introduction to Law Enforcement | 3 | L | - | - | 61% |
| Criminal Justice | 3 | L | Y | - | 52% |
| Fundamentals of Counseling | 3 | L | Y | - | 55% |
| | | | | | |
| **Business:** | | | | | |
| Principles of Finance | 3 | L/U | Y | - | 21% |
| Principles of Financial Accounting | 3 | L | - | Y | 13% |
| Human Resource Management | 3 | L | Y | Y | 69% |
| Organizational Behavior | 3 | L | Y | Y | 47% |
| Principles of Supervision | 3 | L | Y | Y | 67% |
| Business Law II | 3 | L/U | Y | - | 8% |
| Introduction to Computing | 3 | L | Y | - | 86% |
| Introduction to Business | 3 | L | Y | Y | 79% |
| Money & Banking | 3 | L/U | Y | - | 13% |
| Personal Finance | 3 | L | - | Y | 59% |
| Management Information Systems | 3 | L/U | - | - | 77% |
| Business Mathematics | 3 | L | - | Y | 71% |
| | | | | | |
| **Physical Science:** | | | | | |
| Astronomy | 3 | L | - | - | 46% |
| Here's to Your Health | 3 | L | Y | - | 68% |
| Environment & Humanity | 3 | L | Y | - | 59% |
| Principles of Physical Science I | 3 | L | - | - | 46% |
| Physical Geology | 3 | L | - | - | 20% |
| | | | | | |
| **Applied Technology:** | | | | | |
| Technical Writing | 3 | L | Y | - | 80% |
| | | | | | |
| **Humanities:** | | | | | |
| Ethics in America | 3 | L | Y | Y | 65% |
| Introduction to World Religions | 3 | L | Y | - | 59% |
| Principles of Public Speaking | 3 | L | - | - | 85% |

Military pass rates are taken from an old DANTES website, no longer available

L = lower level course (freshman & sophomore)
U = upper level course (junior & senior)

## THOMAS EDISON COLLEGE EXAMINATION PROGRAM (TECEP)
**www.tesc.edu**

Like the Excelsior College examinations described next, TECEP's are offered by one of the accredited independent study institutions, Thomas Edison State College in New Jersey. There are sixty exams that were originally designed only for Thomas Edison students, but now are available to the general public.

For each exam there is a test description that includes an outline of topics covered, a discussion of each topic's relative importance, recommended (or for some tests, required) textbooks, study material and sample questions. Textbooks can be ordered from the College off the website or can usually be found on Amazon or eBay.

Rather than utilizing official institutional or commercial testing sites, TECEP's are taken in the presence of a pre-authorized proctor that you locate on your own. A proctor might be a librarian at a local library or possibly an employee at a college testing or assessment center. Tests can also be taken at military bases or even correctional institutions, just in case.

You must register for the exam, including the request for a certain proctor, at least four weeks before the scheduled exam date. However, you can register for multiple exams on multiple dates with one registration, so you don't to have to worry about that lead time for each one. In other words, you could set up a schedule where you take a test every two weeks, but make your registrations all at one time.

The tests are $62 for students already enrolled in Thomas Edison State College and $124 for non-enrolled students. If you are taking the test at a library, there is normally not a test site charge. However, if you use a college testing center, there may be.

A number score will be sent to the student, but the transcript will only show pass or fail. Failed tests do not show up on the transcript, but you must wait three months to retake. And you can only retake a TECEP exam once.

Finally, many of the courses have optional guided studies, done in a regular sixteen-week format, and self-paced courses that can be done more quickly. However, these courses cost $402 if enrolled in TESC and $624 if not enrolled. Enrolling costs $2,040 the first year and $1,760 in subsequent years. The courses are definitely not required, though, and the majority of students self-study. We will discuss in Chapter 15 the strategies for how and when to enroll if you plan on using Thomas Edison State College as your degree institution.

The list of exams is as follows:

| TECEP Test Title | Credit Hours | Type of Test | Test Length in Hours | Course Available |
|---|---|---|---|---|
| **English Composition:** | | | | |
| English Composition I | 3 | E | 2 | Y |
| English Composition II | 3 | E | 2 | Y |
| | | | | |
| **Humanities:** | | | | |
| Art History I | 3 | M | 2 | Y |
| Art History II | 3 | M | 2 | Y |
| Public Relations Thought & Practice | 3 | M | 3 | - |
| Technical Writing | 3 | E | 4 | Y |
| Introduction to the History of Film | 3 | M | 2 | - |
| Introduction to News Reporting | 3 | E/S | 3 | - |
| Shakespeare I | 3 | E/S | 3 | - |
| Introduction to the Art of Theatre | 3 | M | 2 | - |
| | | | | |
| **Social Sciences:** | | | | |
| Labor Relations & Collective Bargaining | 3 | E/M/S | 3 | - |
| Advanced Labor Relations & Collective Bargaining | 3 | E/S | 3 | - |
| Introduction to Political Science | 3 | M | 2 | - |
| Developmental Psychology | 3 | M | 2 | Y |
| Psychology of Women | 3 | M | 2 | - |
| Thanatology: An Understanding of Death & Dying | 3 | M | 2 | Y |
| Research in Experimental Psychology | 3 | M | 2 | Y |
| Behavior Modification Techniques in Counseling | 3 | M | 2 | - |
| Abnormal Psychology | 3 | M | 2 | Y |
| Psychology of Personality | 3 | M | 2 | Y |
| Organizational Behavior | 3 | M | 2 | - |
| Industrial Psychology | 3 | M | 2 | Y |
| Introduction to Social Psychology | 3 | M | 3 | Y |
| Social Gerontology | 3 | M | 2 | Y |
| Alcohol Abuse: Fundamental Facts | 3 | M | 2 | - |
| Substance Abuse: Fundamental Facts | 3 | M | 2 | - |
| | | | | |
| **Natural Sciences/Mathematics:** | | | | |
| Science of Nutrition | 3 | M | 2 | Y |
| Anatomy & Physiology | 6 | M | 3 | - |
| QBASIC | 3 | M | 3 | - |
| C Programming | 3 | M | 2 | Y |
| BASIC | 3 | M | 3 | - |
| Operating Systems | 3 | M | 2 | Y |

| TECEP Test Title (Continued) | Credit Hours | Type of Test | Test Length in Hours | Course Available |
|---|---|---|---|---|
| Physical Geology | 3 | M | 2 | Y |
| Physics I | 3 | C/M | 3 | Y |
| Physics II | 3 | C.M | 3 | Y |
| Principles of Statistics | 3 | M | 2 | Y |
| | | | | |
| Business: | | | | |
| Federal Income Taxation | 3 | C/M | 3 | Y |
| Business in Society | 3 | E/S/M | 3 | - |
| Business Policy | 3 | E/S/M | 3 | Y |
| Introduction to Computer Information Systems | 3 | M | 2 | - |
| Database Management | 3 | M | 2 | Y |
| Principles of Finance | 3 | M | 3 | Y |
| Security Analysis & Portfolio Management | 3 | M | 2 | - |
| Financial Institutions & Markets | 3 | M | 2 | - |
| International Finance | 3 | C.M | 3 | - |
| Business Law | 3 | M | 2 | Y |
| Principles of Management | 3 | M | 2 | Y |
| Organizational Behavior | 3 | M | 2 | - |
| Labor Relations & Collective Bargaining | 3 | E/M/S | 3 | - |
| Advanced Labor Relations & Collective Bargaining | 3 | E/S | 3 | - |
| Human Resources Management | 3 | M | 2 | Y |
| Introduction to Marketing | 3 | M | 2 | Y |
| Marketing Communications | 3 | E/M | 3 | - |
| Sales Management | 3 | M | 2 | - |
| Advertising | 3 | M | 2 | - |
| Marketing Channels | 3 | E/M | 3 | - |
| Marketing Research | 3 | E/M | 3 | - |
| Marketing Management Strategy | 3 | E | 3 | - |
| Introduction to Operations Management | 3 | M | 3 | Y |
| | | | | |
| Human Services: | | | | |
| Counselor Training: Short-Term Client Systems | 3 | M/O | 2 | - |
| Community Health | 3 | M | 2 | - |
| Introduction to Human Services | 3 | M | 2 | - |
| | | | | |
| Free Electives: | | | | |
| Word Processing Fundamentals | 3 | M | 2 | - |

C = calculations
E = essay
M = multiple choice
O = other
S = short answer

## EXCELSIOR COLLEGE EXAMINATIONS (ECE)
### www.excelsior.edu

ECE exams are offered by Excelsior College, an accredited state college in New York, and one of the independent study institutions mentioned previously. Their tests offer many upper level courses that are not available from CLEP or DANTES. CLEP and DANTES exams are mostly freshman and sophomore level, but ECE and TECEP can fill in the junior and senior level credits for those who wish to take the independent approach all the way through.

Excelsior offers 38 different tests, and the exams are administered at Prometric sites. Prometric is a commercial testing enterprise with sites all around the country. Locations and registration information are available on the web at www.2test.com. They require a minimum of four days lead time, and cost ranges from $165 to $295, depending on the test.

The registration process is a bit complicated, though. First you must register online with Excelsior, then Excelsior will send you an Authorization to Test letter, and only then can you schedule the test with Prometric.

Like CLEP, the tests are done on the computer, and there is on-the-spot grading for most of the exams. The multiple choice tests are graded by the computer while you are still there, but results for what they call their "extended response" tests are mailed later.

You should start by downloading their free Examination Content Guide for each test, found on the website. The Guides give an outline of topics and subtopics the exam will cover and some sample questions. They do not present any material, only a guide for what needs to be studied. They do, however, recommend textbooks for each of the courses.

They also offer Guided Learning Packages for seven tests, which include a course guide, special readings, and optional audio or video materials for between $150 and $225.

Below is a listing of each of their exams along with the type of test:

| ECE<br>Test Title | Credit<br>Hours | Credit<br>Level | Type of<br>Test | Guided<br>Learning<br>Package<br>Available |
|---|---|---|---|---|
| **Arts & Sciences:** | | | | |
| Abnormal Psychology | 3 | U | M | Y |
| American Dream | 6 | U | E | Y |
| Anatomy & Physiology | 6 | L | M | Y |
| English Composition | 6 | L | E | Y |
| Ethics: Theory & Practice | 3 | U | M | Y |
| Foundations of Gerontology | 3 | U | M | - |
| History of Nazi Germany | 3 | U | E | - |
| Life Span Developmental Psychology | 3 | L | M | Y |
| Microbiology | 3 | L | M | Y |
| Organizational Behavior | 3 | U | M | - |
| Pathophysiology | 3 | U | M | - |
| Psychology of Adulthood & Aging | 3 | U | M | - |
| Religions of the World | 3 | U | E | - |
| Research Methods in Psychology | 3 | U | M | - |
| Statistics | 3 | L | M | - |
| World Population | 3 | U | M | - |
| | | | | |
| **Business:** | | | | |
| Ethics: Theory & Practice | 3 | U | M | - |
| Human Resource Management | 3 | U | M | - |
| Labor Relations | 3 | U | M | - |
| Organizational Behavior | 3 | U | M | - |
| | | | | |
| **Education:** | | | | |
| Literacy Instruction in the Elementary | 6 | U | M | - |
| | | | | |
| **Nursing (Associate):** | | | | |
| Fundamentals of Nursing | 8 | L | M | - |
| Maternal & Child Nursing: Associate | 6 | L | M | - |
| Maternity Nursing | 3 | L | M | - |
| Nursing Concepts 1 | 4 | L | M | - |
| Nursing Concepts 2 | 4 | L | M | - |
| Nursing Concepts 3 | 4 | L | M | - |
| Nursing Concepts 4 | 4 | L | M | - |
| Nursing Concepts 5 | 4 | L | M | - |
| Nursing Concepts 6 | 4 | L | M | - |
| Nursing Concepts: Foundations | 4 | L | M | - |
| | | | | |
| **Nursing (Baccalaureate):** | | | | |
| Adult Nursing | 8 | U | M | - |
| Community Health Nursing | 4 | U | M | - |
| Health Support B: Community Health Nsg | 4 | U | M | - |
| Management in Nursing | 4 | U | M | - |
| Maternal & Child Nursing: Baccalaureate | 8 | U | M | - |
| Psychiatric/Mental Health Nursing | 8 | U | M | - |
| Research in Nursing | 3 | U | E/M | - |

L = lower level course (freshman & sophomore)
U = upper level course (junior & senior)

E = extended response
M = multiple choice

## ADVANCED PLACEMENT (AP)
## apcentral.collegeboard.com

Like CLEP exams, Advanced Placement tests are administered by the College Board. They were developed as a cooperative program, giving students the opportunity to take college-level courses in the high school setting. Homeschoolers, however, can sit for the tests without having to take the course.

AP offers 35 tests which are accepted at over 90 percent of colleges and universities. These tests are not as popular as the others for homeschoolers because the tests must be taken at a local high school, but they can still fill a need if your student plans on eventually enrolling in a traditional college. Because many institutions limit the number of the other CBE's accepted, AP's can often be used in addition to these. This allows for more CBE's to be taken and more time and expense saved. You should check with the admissions offices of the colleges you may be interested in to find out their policies.

There is one Christian high school in the St. Louis area that welcomes AP test takers to come on campus and sit for the exam along with their regular students. We do not have any experience with students asking area public schools for permission. We assume they would allow it, but no one we know has ever asked since the Christian school is so accommodating.

Homeschooled students must contact AP Services by March 1 of a given year to ask for a list of AP Coordinators in their area. Then, by March 15, the Coordinator must be contacted. The tests are given in early May with the results available in July. Finally, the tests are multiple choice and "free response," which is either essay or problem solving, and they range in length from two to three hours.

The list of available AP tests follows:

| AP Test Title | Credit Hours |
|---|---|
| Art History | 6 |
| Biology | 8 |
| Calculus AB | 3-4 |
| Calculus BC | 6-8 |
| Chemistry | 8 |
| Computer Science A | 3-4 |
| Computer Science AB | 6-8 |
| Economics: Macro | 3 |
| Economics: Micro | 3 |
| English Language & Composition | 6 |
| English Literature & Composition | 6 |
| Environmental Science | 4 |
| European History | 6 |
| French Language | 6-8 |
| French Literature | 6-12 |
| German Language | 6-8 |
| Government & Politics: Comparative | 3 |
| Government & Politics: United States | 3 |
| Human Geography | - |
| International English Language | - |
| Latin Literature | 6-8 |
| Latin: Vergil | 6-8 |
| Music Theory | 6 |
| Physics B | 6-8 |
| Physics C: Electricity & Magnetism | 4 |
| Physics C: Mechanics | 4 |
| Psychology | 3 |
| Spanish Language | 6-8 |
| Spanish Literature | 6-12 |
| Statistics | 3 |
| Studio Art: 2-D Design | - |
| Studio Art: 3-D Design | - |
| Studio Art: Drawing | 6 |
| U.S. History | 6 |
| World History | - |

To summarize this chapter, the following table reviews the salient points of each testing service:

| | CLEP | DSST | TECEP | ECE | AP |
|---|---|---|---|---|---|
| Number of Tests Offered | 37 | 37 | 60 | 38 | 35 |
| Timed Tests? | Yes, 90 minutes | No time limit | Yes, but varies by test | Yes, 3 hours | Yes, ranging from 2 to 3 hours |
| Computerized Tests? | Yes | No, done on fill-in-the-circle paper forms | No, all on paper and multiple choice questions use fill-in-the-circle forms | Yes | No |
| Instant Results? | Yes | No, results come by mail in 2-4 weeks | No, results come by mail in 4-5 weeks | Yes, if the particular test is multiple choice | No, takes about 7 weeks |
| Multiple Choice? | Yes, five choices except English Comp has optional essay | Yes, four choices | 42 of the 60 tests are completely multiple choice, while some include essays, short answer & calculations | 33 of the 38 tests are completely multiple choice, while the others are "extended response" | Part multiple choice and part "free response" |
| Penalty for Guessing? | No | No | No | No | ¼ point deducted for multiple choice questions answered incorrectly, while no penalty for unanswered questions |

| (Continued) | CLEP | DSST | TECEP | ECE | AP |
|---|---|---|---|---|---|
| Testing Centers | Over 1,300 sites within colleges | About 600 locations, including military bases and college campuses | Tests are taken at an agreed proctor's location, often a library or college | Prometric test centers around the country | In local high schools |
| Take Test Any Time? | Can schedule test at any time, usually with just a few days notice to the test site | Generally two weeks notice so they can order the physical tests | 4 weeks in advance, register with Thomas Edison and recommend a proctor to administer the exam (librarian or college employee) | Must first register with Excelsior, receive an Authorizat'n to Test Letter, and then schedule the test with Prometric | No, only once a year in early May |
| Exam Costs | $55 to CLEP and $15 to test site is common | $60 to DANTES and $20 to test site is common | $62 for Thomas Edison enrolled students, $124 for non-enrolled | $165 to $295 depending on the test | $82 |
| Time Must Wait for Retake if Fail a Test | 6 months | 6 months | 3 months, and can only retake once | 60 days after first failure and 120 after subsequent | One year |
| Must be Enrolled in College? | No | No | No | No | No |
| Number of Colleges that Accept Credits | Nearly 3,000 | Over 1,900 | | Nearly 1,000 | 90% |

In the next chapter we will move from the "what" to the "how," and present some of our thoughts on ways to prepare for these CBE exams so that our young people can begin their college careers. But, a couple additional thoughts may be in order before moving on.

High school students, and even those middle school age, normally would take a test after completing a regular homeschool course. The other method is to grab just one subject at a time, study the material until it is mastered, and then go take the test. After that test is completed, then the next subject is selected and you're off to the races. This is the method used by all our friends who are beyond regular high school age and who want to finish in short order. Most of the subjects can be mastered in two to two and a half weeks by these older students, if working at it full-time.

Assuming a student is starting from scratch with CBE's as a high school graduate, at the above pace your student could earn a degree in fourteen to eighteen months. Some of the tests are six hours, so if we used an average of four hours per test, with the total hours needed to graduate being 120, the total course of study would take between 60 and 75 weeks.

Then, if we assume your child had already earned 30 hours of CBE's while still in their regular high school coursework, and maybe added some dual enrollment credits described in Chapter 13, it would only take an additional 45 to 56 weeks to complete a degree. So, with a good plan and some diligence, a student should be able to finish within a year after high school.

There are no real prizes for finishing quickly, and the pace of study is completely up to each family, but the plan stated above is certainly possible to obtain. But on second thought, maybe there are prizes. What about starting a master's program, seminary, law school or medical school while still under the age of twenty? What about a young man being ready early for marriage and the starting of a new household? What about earning a nice salary three years before his peers? Even if marriage does not follow right away, he could save a nice down payment on a house, or maybe even have enough to buy a house debt-free. And don't forget, no student loan debt with this independent study approach.

# CHAPTER 12

---

## WAYS TO PREPARE
## FOR THE EXAMS

The method or methods you use to prepare for a test will likely be different for each child and each test. At least, that's how it has been for us. The age of the student, and the level of strength in each subject, has an enormous impact on how much effort you will need to apply. Two years ago, our family had three different children prepare and take the History of the U.S. I CLEP exam, and the methods and time invested were very different for all of them. Our son, who was thirteen at the time, definitely worked the hardest, while his sister, a high school senior, simply had to review for a few days.

Since an older child can short circuit some of the steps a younger one has to go through, we thought we would explain the method we use when we work with a younger student trying to master a new subject. And besides, one of the main ideas of the book is to start early.

For our younger students, we begin by using a traditional homeschool textbook to teach the foundations from a biblical perspective. After they have completed the material we have them take a practice test on that subject from the CLEP Official Study Guide, available at any of the chain bookstores. And make sure you always grade the practice test for them, so that they can't see the answers and will be able to take the test again at a future date.

Unfortunately, the practice test often reveals that our younger students need to study more to earn a passing grade. This is where we set out to find them more study material. The amount of new material depends on how well they did on their test. The practice tests will also give us clues as to areas of weakness, and they highlight what subject matter will be emphasized on the exam.

There are many other resources available beyond the homeschool textbook, and every family will find what works best for them. For our family, we have our own favorites. One of our first stops is to our local community college where we search for another textbook on the same subject. Community college textbooks work well, because they seem to be written in an understandable way for our younger students. You don't necessarily have to study the entire book, though. Simply going over areas of weakness and reviewing terms in the glossary is often enough.

You have to be a bit cautious of the content, because it is secular, but for some subjects such as science, you will probably need to learn these worldly concepts to do well on the exams. For Astronomy, our fourteen year old studied a homeschool text, but then also read a community college book. He obviously had to endure the "billions of years" lie, but sadly some of that material was on the exam.

Another method of study we utilize is Test Prep Guides. These are tremendously helpful for narrowing what needs to be mastered. They boil down the text and review the most important pieces of information. They often contain practice tests with lengthy explanations of why an answer is right or wrong. Keep in mind as well that if a subject is relatively easy, but not exactly pure, such as Psychology, this book alone could replace the textbook entirely. It will only highlight main themes and avoid impure details.

A couple of our family's other favorite tools, described later in this chapter, include the online InstantCert Academy and the laminated Subject Charts available at most bookstores.

After all this, depending on the level of review needed, they retake their practice test from the CLEP Official Study Guide and see how they do. We have found the practice tests to be an incredibly accurate guide as to how well they will perform on the actual test.

They usually score one or two points higher on the CLEP test than they do on the practice test.

Please don't feel overwhelmed by the amount of material you may need to use, though. It's actually quite fun! Besides, the older and more experienced your child becomes, the faster and more easily they will be able to prepare for the next one. Last year, our son, who was a junior in high school, decided to study for one subject a month and then take a CBE. Although he began much more slowly a year or two before, he became better at mastering each subject as he grew older. He is also interning for a State Senator and working at our bookstore, so you can see it's really not that hard once you learn the system.

There are endless ways to learn and master material, though. This approach has worked for us so far, but we may find a better way tomorrow. So, here is an explanation of the different material categories and various sources to consider for your family.

### TEXTBOOKS

As we have said, for most CBE's, unless the student already has a good understanding of a particular subject, he will need to find an information source for the bulk of the material. A good textbook, as the underlying foundation, is probably the most common method for learning the basics.

The textbook may be part of a regular high school curriculum. The student would take a CLEP or DANTES test after completing a homeschool course. He may still want to look over a test prep guide and/or do some practice tests, but most of the material will be gleaned from the regular semester or year-long course.

If your student studies American History in his homeschool high school, you can utilize some of the other tools if needed, sign him up for a CLEP test when he's done, and go get three, or even six, hours of college credit. And don't forget that the exam only costs $70 and therefore only $23.33 per credit hour (or $11.67 if it is a six hour credit exam). This compares to around $500 per credit for even an inexpensive private college. And as we have said before, your highschooler will also be invigorated by the idea of earning college credit while still in twelfth, eleventh, tenth, ninth or even eighth grade. Our third child, Joe, took his first test in seventh grade. He barely passed, but he did pass. They're all pass-fail, so a pass is a pass!

Good subjects for this approach (taking a CBE after completion of a homeschool high school course) that match well with CLEP tests are American Government, American History, Economics, Composition, Algebra, Trigonometry, Biology, Chemistry and Foreign Languages.

The other approach mentioned above is to look for a textbook at a local college. We prefer community college bookstores because their books will normally be more easily comprehended by a student high school age, yet still cover the subject well.

## TEST PREP GUIDES

Now we're moving beyond the learning of the foundational material to some of the tools and guides that can be used during final preparation. We recommend using a test prep guide for most all of the courses, as they cover the most important concepts in a quick and concise manner. And most of them will also include practice tests. A test prep guide is much like the CliffsNotes those "other" students used when you were in high school. They summarize a subject and highlight what they believe to be the most essential points to study in preparation for a test. In fact, "ol' Cliff" is still around and produces study guides that you can use for this purpose.

As indicated above, for the student who already has some general knowledge about a subject, a textbook could be skipped, and he could go straight to the test preps. They are complete enough for this type of student, as well as older students who have been around the block a few times. They will not provide nearly as much detail or depth as a textbook, but for just gleaning what needs to be known, they could suffice as the main source of information.

We recommend the following publishers, which are also summarized at the end of this chapter showing all CLEP study helps in one chart. That chart will include the Test Prep Guides, Subject Charts, Flashcards, Practice Tests, and Other Tools. For now, here are descriptions of each publisher's test prep guides:

1) Research and Education Association (www.rea.com) – REA publishes several helps that can be used as test prep. They offer review handbooks specifically for CLEP preparation for the five general exams plus twelve other tests. Each of these preps can be purchased with or without their TESTware CD-ROM, which includes two of the three included practice tests.

   We like the REA CLEP guides because they provide a good deal of material to study, along with practice tests and test answers, to make sure you have it down. The only unfortunate part is that they currently produce guides for just seventeen of the thirty seven exams. As with each of these preps, the exams they cover are shown on the chart at the end of the chapter.

   In addition to the CLEP reviews, though, REA publishes two other guides: Super Reviews and Essentials. The Super Reviews provide study material related to a certain subject and with numerous problems, solutions, exercises and quizzes, help you master a given course. The Essentials series is about a third the size of the Super Reviews and gives a more concise summary of the subject at hand. Super Reviews match up with fourteen CLEP's and the Essentials with eighteen.

   Finally, even though the AP tests are not the same as CLEP, many publishers, including REA, produce AP prep guides and can be used as good material for CLEP preparation (remember, CLEP and AP are both administered by the College Board). REA produces thirteen AP guides that fit with the CLEP subjects.

2)  CliffsNotes Reviews (www.cliffsnotes.com) –
    The CliffsNotes company publishes a few different types of guides that can be of help, including CliffsQuickReview, CliffsStudySolver and CliffsAP. The QuickReview covers the essentials of a topic and also offers chapter summaries and review questions. The StudySolver is about 20 percent review material using tables, graphs and diagrams and 80 percent practice problems. The AP guides give a review of key concepts, along with practice exams and detailed answers.

3)  Peterson's CLEP Guides (www.petersons.com) –
    Peterson's offers two guides, CLEP Success and Master the CLEP. CLEP Success covers all five general exams, with each chapter offering a pre-test, a subject overview, and then a post-test. It also contains two full-length practice tests on paper, with answers and explanations, and two more on CD-ROM. Master the CLEP also provides practice tests for each of the five general exams, but in addition, it gives an overview of all the other CLEP tests. Peterson's also sells a DANTES guide that covers eight subjects with review material, pre- and post-tests, and full-length practice exams.

4)  Barron's AP Guides (www.barronseduc.com) –
    These guides include subject review, questions at the end of each section, glossary of terms, and full-length practice exams with questions answered.

5)  Teaching Solutions (www.teachingsolutions.org) –
    This organization sells downloadable teaching material for nearly all the CLEP tests. The cost is around $50 for each subject.

6) National Learning Corp. Passbooks (www.passbooks.com) – This company produces a Passbook for every CLEP test. In addition, they have books for DSST and ECE. They are not downloadable, though, and must be ordered online and shipped. They run around $30 each.

7) CLEP Official Study Guide (www.collegeboard.com) – The College Board, the administrators of the CLEP, publishes the official guide to all the tests. The book contains approximately fifty sample questions and answers for each CLEP, along with some test-taking tips. It does not contain any review material. The individual subject portions of the Guide can be purchased and downloaded off the website if you are only planning to take a few tests.

8) Other – There are several other helpful prep guides that can be found at a local bookstore. Kaplan, for instance, has nine AP guides that line up with CLEP's, and there are others.

## SUBJECT CHARTS

There are three publishers that attempt to summarize an entire course's most important material in a folded, laminated 8½ by 11 inch chart. These are very helpful and provide a great last stop for test preparation. It's amazing what they can cram into such a small space.

QuickStudy Charts are normally available at Borders and also at www.quickstudy.com. Spark Charts can be found at Barnes & Noble and at www.sparknotes.com. Finally, REA Charts can be found at a few bookstores and online at www.rea.com.

## Flashcards

REA makes a series of flashcards and the Sparks Charts company also makes Spark Study Cards. These are available online at www.rea.com and www.sparknotes.com, respectively.

## Practice Tests

Our children have found the use of practice tests very helpful, and there are many places to find them. Most of the Test Prep Guides already mentioned include practice tests. In addition, Peterson's has online practice tests for CLEP at www.petersons.com. For each available subject, they offer three tests. The cost is $20 for ninety days of access.

## Other Tools

There are also other miscellaneous tools that might be of help:

1) InstantCert Academy (www.instantcertonline.com) – This is a very interesting online CLEP prep service. It does not provide any traditional content, but it asks a series of questions designed to teach you the material as you go through. It might ask you once, "The father of communism is _____." And if you don't know it would tell you the answer is Karl Marx. Then, later, it might ask, "Karl Marx is the father of _____." By asking the question in multiple ways, it reinforces the learning.

The cost is $20 per month, but the service can be cancelled and started up again at any time. They currently offer twenty CLEP courses and twenty DANTES courses. They seem to be adding more all the time, though.

2) Free University Project (www.freeuniv.com) –
   The creator of this website gives the user an outline for several CLEP subjects and what to study to pass the tests. He then has links to free sources of all the information. It is definitely worth checking out. They also have some DSST subjects.

3) Houghton Mifflin (college.hmco.com/students) –
   This site has some very helpful tools including free online practice tests and interactive flashcards. The flashcards are especially interesting, as they show a term and then flip the card when you are ready for the answer. It also allows you to check a box on an individual card, indicating that you have learned it, so that it stops coming up. You can also shuffle the pack. Unfortunately, the only subjects available that line up with CLEP are accounting, chemistry, economics, humanities, management, marketing, psychology, and the languages.

We now bring you to the chart referenced earlier. It summarizes many of the test prep helps in one matrix. At first glance it may seem overwhelming, but with a little orientation you should be able to look at a particular CLEP test and see what helps are available.

It will take some time to determine for your student what works best and what is within your budget. For the first test or two you may want to order several of the helps to see what they are like. Then, as you become more experienced, you will learn what is most worthwhile and only have to buy your favorites in the future.

Also, there are other helps that are either designed specifically for, or will work well with, the other testing services. Especially for DANTES, there are specific prep guides available. In the interest of space, though, we have only included CLEP in the chart. In addition, CLEP is our focus at this point because most students will start there and by the time you hit the others, you will be an expert. Trust us on that one!

## CLEP Preparation Tools Chart

| Subject | REA (C=CLEP Guide, S=Super Review, E=Essentials, A=AP Guide, N=EXAMNotes, F=Flashcard Books) | Cliffs (Q=QuickReview, S=StudySolver, A=AP Guide) | Peterson's (S=CLEP Success, M=Master CLEP, A=AP Guide, O=Online Practice Tests) | Barron's (A=AP Guide) | Passbooks (C=CLEP) | Spark/Bar (S=SparkNotes, C=SparkNotes Study Cards, Q=QuickStudy Charts) | Instant Cert (I=Available InstantCert Subject) | Free University (F=Free University Subject) | Teaching Solutions (T=Teaching Solutions Subject) |
|---|---|---|---|---|---|---|---|---|---|
| **General:** | | | | | | | | | |
| College Mathematics | C | - | S/M/O | - | C | - | I | F | T |
| English Composition (w/essay) | C/A/N | - | S/M/O | A | C | S/Q | - | F | T |
| Humanities | C | - | S/M/O | - | C | - | I | F | T |
| Natural Sciences | C | - | S/M/O | - | C | - | I | F | T |
| Social Sciences & History | C | - | S/M/O | - | C | - | I | F | T |
| **History & Social Sciences:** | | | | | | | | | |
| American Government | A | Q/A | A/O | A | C | S/Q | I | F | T |
| Human Growth & Development | C | - | O | - | C | - | I | - | T |
| History of the US I | C/E/A/N/F | Q/A | A/O | A | C | S/C/Q | I | F | T |
| History of the US II | C/E/A/N/F | Q/A | A/O | A | C | S/C/Q | I | F | T |
| Introduction to Educational Psych | - | - | O | - | C | - | I | - | - |
| Introductory Psychology | C/S/E/A/N | Q | O | A | C | S/Q | I | F | T |
| Introductory Sociology | C/S/E/N | Q | O | - | C | S/Q | I | F | T |
| Macroeconomics | S/A/N/F | Q/A | O | A | C | S/Q | I | F | T |
| Microeconomics | S/A/N/F | Q/A | O | A | C | S/Q | I | F | T |
| Western Civilization I | - | - | O | - | C | S/Q | I | F | T |
| Western Civilization II | - | - | O | - | C | S/Q | I | F | T |
| **Composition & Literature:** | | | | | | | | | |
| American Literature | - | - | O | - | C | Q | - | F | T |
| Analyzing & Interpreting Literature | C | - | O | - | C | - | - | - | T |
| English Literature | - | - | - | A | C | Q | - | - | T |
| Freshman College Composition | C/S/A/N | - | O | - | C | S/Q | - | F | T |
| **Science & Mathematics:** | | | | | | | | | |
| Calculus with Elementary Functions | S/E/A/N | Q/A | A | A | C | S/Q | - | - | T |
| College Algebra | C/N | Q/S | O | - | C | S/Q | - | F | T |
| College Algebra/Trigonometry | S/E/N | Q | - | - | C | S/Q | - | - | T |

| CLEP Preparation Tools Chart (Continued) | REA<br>C = CLEP Guide<br>S = Super Review<br>E = Essentials<br>A = AP Guide<br>N = EXAMNotes<br>F = Flashcard Books | Cliffs<br>Q = QuickReview<br>S = StudySolver<br>A = AP Guide | Peterson's<br>S = CLEP Success<br>M = Master CLEP<br>A = AP Guide<br>O = Online<br>Practice Tests | Barron's<br>A = AP Guide | Passbooks<br>C = CLEP | Spark/Bar<br>S = SparkNotes<br>C = SparkNotes<br>Study Cards<br>Q = QuickStudy<br>Charts | Instant Cert<br>I = Available<br>InstantCert<br>Subject | Free University<br>F = Free<br>University Subject | Teaching Solutions<br>T = Teaching<br>Solutions Subject |
|---|---|---|---|---|---|---|---|---|---|
| General Biology | C/S/E/A/N/F | Q/S/A | O | A | C | S/C/Q | I | F | T |
| General Chemistry | S/E/A/N/F | Q/S/A | A/O | A | C | S/C/Q | - | F | T |
| Trigonometry | N | Q/S | - | - | C | S/Q | - | - | T |
| Business: | | | | | | | | | |
| Introductory Accounting | S/E/N | Q | O | - | C | S/Q | I | - | - |
| Introductory Business Law | E/N | - | - | - | C | S/Q | I | - | T |
| Information Systems/Computers | E | Q | O | A | C | Q | I | - | T |
| Principles of Management | E | - | O | - | C | S/Q | I | - | T |
| Principles of Marketing | C | - | - | - | C | S/Q | I | - | T |
| Foreign Language: | | | | | | | | | |
| College French I | S/E/N/F | Q | - | A | C | S/Q | - | F | T |
| College French II | S/E/N/F | Q | - | A | C | S/Q | - | F | T |
| College German I | E/N/F | - | - | - | C | S/Q | - | F | T |
| College German II | E/N/F | - | - | - | C | S/Q | - | F | T |
| College Spanish I | C/S/E/A/N/F | Q/S/A | O | A | C | S/C/Q | - | F | T |
| College Spanish II | C/S/E/A/N/F | Q/S | O | A | C | S/C/Q | - | F | T |

# CHAPTER 13

---

# DUAL
# ENROLLMENT

Dual enrollment courses are college classes offered to high school students, normally on a college campus, and the student can simultaneously earn credit at both levels. The majority of higher education institutions now offer this opportunity. It is normally open to students in their junior and senior years of high school, but exceptions are sometimes made for younger students. These are the same courses taken by traditional college-age students, and high school students simply join their regular class.

If you believe a classroom environment would be beneficial for your student for a particular subject, this is a good way to go. For instance, if your child's planned college degree will require a lab with one or more sciences, taking the class during high school through dual enrollment may save you both time and money. Or maybe you would want your student to take an actual course in their prospective major in order to get a little extra grounding and to have the help of a professor. Some parents simply want their child to gain the experience of being in a classroom environment while still in the home setting for the bulk of the high school courses.

Also, if you are not planning on taking the independent study approach all the way through, the institution to which you would be transferring may limit the number of CBE's accepted. This makes dual enrollment a good alternative to earn some extra credits before traditional college age. While most institutions will only let the student take one or two classes per semester, a student who really wants to take advantage of this method will enroll with more than one college, taking two at each.

The colleges we have worked with for dual enrollment have been exceedingly helpful. They ask us to prepare a summary of the subjects taught in high school from ninth grade on. The summary usually would include the semester, the course, the curriculum used, and a grade. We assign each class an "A", because with the tutoring method we don't move on until the material is mastered. You may have a more formal grading system, and you can use that.

We then make an appointment with the admissions department of the college to meet us and the prospective student. Often there will be one counselor assigned for all dual enrollment students, so you will want to ask specifically for them. At the meeting, it is our experience that they will go over the high school course summary and ask the student some general questions about their academic and career goals. They will also be looking for a maturity level sufficient to take on a college level course.

You should not be intimidated by this process at all. The interviews we have had have been very relaxed. Both sides want to make it work out, and since with homeschooling there is no concrete academic record, it becomes a very subjective process. The college just wants to get a feel for the student's character and initiative.

So, what are the advantages of dual enrollment, as opposed to taking the same course after reaching traditional college age?

1) Price –
   Most local colleges and universities charge less per credit hour for their dual enrolled students than their traditional students. The most popular dual enrollment school in St. Louis gives a 78 percent discount. They believe it is a good recruitment tool to get prospective students on campus and experience campus life, so they give us a break.

2) Admissions Are Much Easier –
As mentioned above, the only admissions criteria we have seen is an informal summary of high school coursework, a brief interview so that the admissions counselor can judge the student's maturity level, and a check for the tuition. And if you already have some CBE credits, it can make the process even easier.

3) No ACT or SAT Tests –
Because your student would not be an "incoming freshman," most colleges do not require admissions tests. They look at dual enrollers outside their normal box. However, we have been hearing that this may change in the future at some institutions.

4) Establish a Grade Point Average –
Since the CBE testing services do not issue grades, and dual enrollment classes do, you may want to try a dual enrollment class or two, so that a GPA will be established. Especially if you are planning on using the blended approach (starting with CBE's and dual enrollment and later transferring to a traditional college), having an established GPA attached to your name might be helpful during a later admissions process.

Some disadvantages of dual enrollment, instead of using all CBE's:

1) They Still Cost More than CBE's –
A dual enrollment course may be $300, or often much more, while CLEP's are only $70.

2) They Still Take a Full Semester to Complete –
It is a traditional classroom course, so there will be a lot of wasted time.

3) They Still Take Away Flexibility –
   The classes run on schedule, and the assignments and tests are due when they are due. Homeschoolers are used to more flexibility, and the professors probably are not in a position to make many exceptions.

4) There Still is the Possibility of a Compromised Environment –
   Both from the perspective of impure students and of getting a liberal or carnal professor, sending them into a class takes away, to some degree, your ability to know what is going on. Since it is local, and therefore an institution you will likely have some familiarity with, the risk is less, but it certainly still exists. Also, since it is only one or two classes, the likelihood of being led astray is certainly lessened.

Our experience with dual enrollment is that we have not had any major concerns we couldn't work through. At a local Christian college, we saw some composition assignments that were inappropriate for any institution, but we talked it through with our child and will stay away from that professor in the future if any of our other children take a class there.

By the way, Liberty University offers distance, dual enrollment courses. It is still $210 per credit hour, but there are some subjects that would fit very well in this arrangement. English Composition I and II, for example, might be great courses to take this way. In addition, Patrick Henry College does not have an age requirement for their distance courses, so these could function just like dual enrollment. Both of these are potentially good options if you are uncomfortable sending a younger student to class with college freshmen.

In the end, dual enrollment is another tool in your belt and can be a good supplement to the fully independent study method or for gathering further non-traditional credit hours when a blended approach is planned.

# CHAPTER 14

---

# A FEW
# MORE TOOLS

CBE's and dual enrollment are by far the most popular tools among homeschoolers to begin accumulating college credits. There are, however, other sources that should not be overlooked:

1) Professional, Continuing Education
2) Distance Learning
3) Portfolio Assessment

### PROFESSIONAL, CONTINUING EDUCATION

The American Council on Education (ACE) issues a publication each year, the current one being entitled, *2004-2005 National Guide to Educational Credit for Training Programs*. The purpose of the Guide is to "help adults obtain academic credit for formal courses taken outside college and university degree programs."[43] These options work very well within the independent study model and can let the student gain credit for courses that may also help with their continuing education later on the job.

This huge, almost two thousand page Guide, lists organization after organization offering training courses for their own employees, for members of associations, or in the case of training suppliers, their customers. ACE then recommends the number of hours of college credit a course deserves, as well as its level.

For example, my (Scott's) field is insurance, and I have completed the Associate in Risk Management (ARM) designation from the American Institute for Chartered Property Casualty Underwriters, Insurance Institute of America. The Guide shows a description of each of the three exams required for the designation and then recommends that each course be granted three semester hours of upper division baccalaureate or graduate degree credit in Business Administration, Insurance, Management or Risk Management. If I had known about this and taken these courses while I was still in college, I could have earned nine hours of credit toward my business major.

Now, not every college and university accepts these credits, but the independent study institutions normally do. That is the reason we are describing these at this point. As you are planning your studies, assuming you have a good idea of the field you are planning to pursue, it might be a good idea to try and find some of these courses to take as either electives within your major or just as free electives. That way you might have already earned a professional designation upon graduation that would be very impressive to any prospective employer.

Just a small sampling of the more than three hundred organizations offering courses that have been evaluated by ACE include:

American Academy of Nutrition
American Bankers Association
American Management Association
American Society of Safety Engineers
Appraisal Institute
Center for Financial Training
Certified Credit Union Executive Program
Certified Employee Benefit Specialist Program
Educational Institute of the American Hotel & Lodging Assoc.

Institute of Logistical Management
Institute of Management and Production
Insurance Institute of America
Mortgage Bankers Association of America
U.S. Dept's of Defense, Agriculture, Energy, Justice, Personnel
U.S. Postal Service

We were not able to find a complete list of courses evaluated by ACE online, so the only way we know to find the information is to order the hardcopy book. It is not cheap, at $105, but the information could prove to be very helpful. The book can be ordered through ACE's online bookstore at www.acenet.edu.

Before you order the Guide, though, you should ask the institution through which you plan to graduate to make sure they accept most of the courses listed by ACE. Again, the independent study institutions normally will, but if you are thinking of a blended approach, beginning with independent study and switching later to a traditional college, you will want to know if they accept these credits before going too far down the road.

## DISTANCE LEARNING

Distance learning has been booming over the past several years. You can find thousands of accredited courses online, on video and CD, or through other correspondence vehicles. There certainly is no shortage of resources.

The only problem with these courses is that they normally cost about the same as a classroom-based program. That being said, though, they still may be a good option for a student planning on a blended approach. Most of the institutions offering courses will issue grades, and as long as they are accredited, they potentially could be transferred to a student's graduating college. And, as with dual enrollment, the credits would normally be in addition to any CBE limitations imposed by a traditional college.

So, taking some extra distance learning still keeps the student at home, but extra credits could be earned. Again, it still is expensive, but it may fill a needed role, especially for a tougher subject that a student is uncomfortable handling through CBE.

Distance learning courses come in self-paced packages, or courses may follow a regular semester with very traditional college assignments like papers, quizzes and tests. Shorter courses are also becoming more popular.

The learning can be done with or without help from a professor or advisor, and there may or may not be contact with other students. These things can obviously be pros or cons depending on your situation.

Also, the technology varies widely. Some courses are completely internet-based, with both content and testing on a web platform. On the other end of the continuum, a course may consist merely of a printed syllabus and maybe some videos, with papers and exams being mailed to the college for grading.

In summary, this approach will not likely be part of your plans unless it is a subject in which you simply have a great deal of interest or is maybe a critical part of your major and you desire some extra support. But we wanted to at least have a brief discussion here, because it is such a growing part of today's education environment.


## PORTFOLIO ASSESSMENT

Our first orientation to this whole idea of doing college a different way came from a seminar we attended a few years ago. It was put on by Global Learning Strategies, founded by Brad Voeller. He published a book in 2002 called *Accelerated Distance Learning*, and it has been a valuable resource for us.

One of the concepts he introduced was Portfolio Assessment, or, as some colleges call it, Prior Learning Assessment. These types of credits are accepted by many colleges and universities around the country and definitely by the first two of the three independent study schools described in the next chapter.

So, what is Portfolio Assessment? In short, it is asking for college credit for knowledge gleaned from life experience. You just need to prove you received college-level learning from that experience. The proof is normally in the form of a narrative document whose form may be prescribed, or it may be open to the student's creativity. Either way, the college will most likely have established guidelines.

Some schools will want the submission to be a process over time with the help of a mentor, while others will take a submission at any time. The Thomas Edison State College website (www.tesc.edu) has a thorough discussion of what they expect. It is under Prospective Students, then Undergraduate Programs, then Ways to Earn Credit, then Prior Learning Assessment, then PLA Process.

Brad Voeller offers a very helpful five-step process to producing a professional portfolio:[44]

1) Identify Your Areas of Learning –
   Think back over the last several years and try to identify some life experiences that may have produced college-level learning. These experiences may have come through employment, church, politics, hobbies, volunteer work, seminars or workshops, reading, art, etc. Again, the key is whether or not the learning is at the college level. The learning could also come from something you haven't done yet, but plan to do.

2) Identify a College Course that is Equivalent to Your Learning Experience –
   You normally can't just make up a course to fit your experiences. It must match something the college, or other colleges, offer. After identifying the course you wish to use, try to find a course description in a catalog.

3) Make Sure that the Credit for the Course You Have Selected Fits Into Your Degree Program –
You wouldn't want to go through all this work if the course won't count toward your degree.

4) Describe Your Learning Experience in a Narrative –
Brad Voeller recommends contacting an advisor first before starting your narrative to make sure it will include what is required. It should answer questions like how, where, when, what, who, and why? Also, the narrative should follow the course description you found, and it should show how your life experience has covered each topic.

5) Present Evidence that Documents and Verifies the Learning –
In addition to the narrative, you must be able to substantiate your experience. This might be done through samples of work, certificates, test results, reports, licenses, letters, awards, media clippings, photos, programs, etc.

Now, just a couple more things to keep in mind. The first is that a school may still charge their regular credit hour rate for the portfolio assessment. And the second is that you normally cannot submit an assessment for a subject covered by a CBE. Colleges believe the CBE's are a better judge of a student's subject mastery, so if you have the knowledge, why not just go take the test.

# CHAPTER 15

---

# WHO OFFERS THIS
# TYPE OF DEGREE PROGRAM?

There are three fully accredited colleges that offer a purely, or almost purely, independent study degree. These are Thomas Edison State College of New Jersey, Charter Oak State College of Connecticut, and Excelsior College of New York. Together, many have referred to these as the "Big Three."

As we have discussed previously, there are numerous colleges that offer online degrees. But these will almost always involve similar expense to a brick-and-mortar campus and are usually done along with a group of students and an instructor over a fixed period, so you can't work at your own pace. Some do offer self-paced courses, but the vast majority involve online interaction with the instructor and other students for a prescribed number of weeks, much like a regular classroom situation.

From a cost standpoint, the largest online provider of degrees, the University of Phoenix, still charges $460 per credit hour for undergraduate courses. This is over $55,000 for the degree, but the independent study institutions are much less. Again, a fully accredited bachelor's degree can be achieved for about $6,000.

## THOMAS EDISON STATE COLLEGE
**www.tesc.edu**

Founded in 1972 with a mission to serve the adult learner, Thomas Edison State College (TESC) is one of the twelve state colleges of New Jersey. They believed that the "college-level knowledge adults gain outside the classroom could be measured and applied toward an academic degree."[45] They offer a good variety of associate, bachelors and master's degrees in more than one hundred areas of study. The College was named after inventor Thomas Alva Edison, who was from New Jersey, and gained his vast knowledge without attending college classes.

TESC's mission is to allow college credit from an array of sources and methods in order to make a degree accessible to more and more learners. They allow credit from the following:

1) Their Own Guided Study or Online Courses –
   These involve regular semester coursework and regular communications with faculty mentors and fellow students. Assignments are given, tests and quizzes administered, papers assigned, topics discussed via email, etc. The courses are very similar to a classroom experience, only at a distance from your home. The cost, however, is not much less than a traditional college.

2) Their Own e-Pack® Courses –
   TESC also offers online instruction without following a typical semester course format. These involve the study of chapters, followed by taking quizzes at your own pace, and then taking a final exam whenever you are ready. Cost is equivalent to the courses above.

3) Standardized Tests –
   The College accepts all of the Credit by Examination testing services (CLEP, DSST, TECEP, ECE and AP), and you can earn a degree almost entirely through CBE.

4) Prior Learning Assessment –
   This is TESC's name for Portfolio Assessment, and they will accept credits in this manner. Their suggested sources of knowledge include full or part-time jobs, independent reading and study, training program or in-service courses, volunteer work, cultural and artistic pursuits, hobbies and recreational pastimes, community or religious activities, military service, travel study, and organizational memberships.

5) ACE-Approved Courses –
   As mentioned in the prior chapter, there are many professional courses offered that will equate to credit at the College.

6) Military Training –
   The College will grant credit for military service school courses that have been evaluated by ACE's Office on Educational Credit.

7) Approved Correspondence Courses –
   They are not very specific about what may qualify in this category, but are obviously open to a prospective student asking.

8) Credit for Licenses and Certificates –
   TESC's website lists several licenses and certificates eligible for credit.

9) Credits Earned at Other Accredited Colleges –
As with most colleges and universities, you can transfer in course credit you have received at another institution. This would also apply to any dual enrollment you may have done.

The following tables show the degrees TESC offers along with the related majors. In the case of the associate degrees, the majors are called "options," for the baccalaureate they are referred to as "major areas of study," and for the masters an individual course of study is a "focus."

| TESC ASSOCIATE DEGREES |
| --- |
| Associate in Applied Science (AAS)<br>    Administrative Studies<br>    Applied Computer Studies<br>    Applied Electronic Studies<br>    Applied Health Studies<br>    Mechanics and Maintenance<br>    Occupational Studies<br><br>Associate in Science in Management (ASM)<br>    Accounting<br>    Administrative Office Management<br>    Banking<br>    Computer Information Systems<br>    Finance<br>    General Management<br>    Hospital Health Care Administration<br>    Hotel/Motel/Restaurant Management<br>    Human Resources Management<br>    Insurance<br>    International Business<br>    Marketing<br>    Operations Management<br>    Procurement<br>    Public Administration<br>    Purchasing and Materials Management<br>    Real Estate<br>    Retailing Management<br>    Small Business Management/Entrepreneurship<br>    Transportation/Distribution Management<br><br>Associate in Science in Applied Science and Technology (ASAST)<br>    Air Traffic Control<br>    Architectural Design<br>    Aviation Flight Technology<br>    Aviation Maintenance Technology |

**TESC ASSOCIATE DEGREES (Continued)**

Biomedical Electronics
Civil and Construction Engineering Technology
Clinical Laboratory Science
Computer Science Technology
Dental Hygiene
Electrical Technology
Electronics Engineering Technology
Engineering Graphics
Environmental Sciences
Fire Protection Science
Forestry
Horticulture
Laboratory Animal Science
Manufacturing Engineering Technology
Marine Engineering Technology
Mechanical Engineering Technology
Nondestructive Testing Technology
Nuclear Engineering Technology
Nuclear Medicine Technology
Radiation Protection
Radiation Therapy
Respiratory Care
Surveying

Associate in Arts (AA)

Associate in Science in Natural Sciences and Mathematics (ASNSM)
Biology
Computer Science
Mathematics

Associate in Science in Public and Social Services (ASPSS)
Administration of Justice
Child Development Services
Community Services
Emergency Disaster Management
Fitness & Wellness Services
Gerontology
Legal Services
Recreation Services
Social Services
Social Services for Special Populations

**TESC BACCALAUREATE DEGREES**

Bachelor of Arts (BA)
*Humanities*
Art
Communications
English

**TESC BACCALAUREATE DEGREES (Continued)**

Foreign Language
Journalism
Humanities
Music
Philosophy
Photography
Religion
Theater Arts
*Social Sciences/History*
Anthropology
Economics
History
Labor Studies
Political Science
Psychology
Social Sciences/History
Sociology
*Natural Sciences/Mathematics*
Biology
Computer Science
Mathematics
Natural Sciences/Mathematics
*Interdisciplinary*
Environmental Studies
Liberal Studies

Bachelor of Science in Applied Science and Technology (BSAST)
Air Traffic Control
Architectural Design
Aviation Flight Technology
Aviation Maintenance Technology
Biomedical Electronics
Civil Engineering Technology
Clinical Laboratory Science
Computer Science Technology
Construction
Cytotechnology
Dental Hygiene
Electrical Technology
Electronics Engineering Technology
Engineering Graphics
Environmental Sciences
Fire Protection Science
Forestry
Horticulture
Laboratory Animal Science
Manufacturing Engineering Technology
Marine Engineering Technology
Mechanical Engineering Technology
Medical Imaging
Nondestructive Testing Technology
Nuclear Engineering Technology
Nuclear Medicine Technology
Perfusion Technology

**TESC BACCALAUREATE DEGREES (Continued)**

Radiation Protection
Radiation Therapy
Respiratory Care
Surveying

Bachelor of Science in Business Administration (BSBA)
Accounting
Administrative Office Management
Advertising Management
Banking
Computer Information Systems
Finance
General Management
Hospital Health Care Administration
Hotel/Motel/Restaurant Management
Human Resources Management
Insurance
International Business
Logistics
Marketing
Operations Management
Organizational Management
Procurement
Public Administration
Purchasing and Materials Management
Real Estate
Retailing Management
Small Business Management/Entrepreneurship
Transportation/Distribution Management

Bachelor of Science in Health Sciences (BSHeS)
Allied Dental Education
Dietetic Sciences
Imaging Sciences

Bachelor of Science in Human Services (BSHS)
Administration of Justice
Child Development Services
Community Services
Emergency Disaster Management
Gerontology
Health and Nutrition Counseling
Health Services
Health Services Administration
Health Services Education
Legal Services
Mental Health and Rehabilitative Services
Recreation Services
Social Services
Social Services Administration
Social Services for Special Populations

Bachelor of Science in Nursing (BSN)

| TESC MASTER'S DEGREES |
| --- |
| Master of Science in Human Resources Management (MSHRM)<br><br>Master of Science in Management (MSM)<br>    Insurance<br>    Management of Substance Abuse Programs<br>    Project Management<br>    Public Sector Auditing<br><br>Master of Arts in Professional Studies (MAPS) |

The vast majority of the credits in each of these majors can be earned by CBE. For us, that is what we are looking for because the costs stay very low and it allows our children to work completely at their own pace.

To get started, we would recommend downloading the Program Planning Handbook. From the TESC home page, click on Enrollment Information, then click on College Catalog, then you can download the Handbook. It contains the general guidelines, by degree, that you will need to begin planning your student's program, such as deciding what CBE's to start taking, and the non-CBE coursework that may be required.

In addition to the Handbook, you will need to find the Area of Study Guide Sheet for the applicable major. On the home page, start with Prospective Students, then Undergraduate Programs on the left, then Degree Programs. It will list all the degrees, and then you can find any major under the degrees from there.

As an example, let's look at a Bachelor of Arts Degree in Political Science. Using the Program Planning Handbook section entitled Bachelor of Arts (page 64 in the 2005-2006 edition), the Area of Study Guide Sheet for Political Science, and the listings of the different CBE tests in Chapter 11 of this book, you can determine all the different options for completing this major.

The following chart shows one possible path for completing the 120 credit hours needed for graduation:

| SAMPLE DEGREE PATH USING A B.A. IN POLITICAL SCIENCE FROM TESC | | |
| --- | --- | --- |
| **Subject Category** | **Credits** | **Examples of Possible Credit Sources** |
| **General Education Requirements** | 60 | |
| English Composition | 6 | CLEP English Comp w/Essay (6) |
| Humanities | 12 | CLEP Analyzing & Interpreting Literature (6)<br>DSST Ethics in America (3)<br>DSST Principles of Public Speaking (3) |
| Social Sciences<br>(Macroeconomics must be 3 of<br>the hours) | 12 | CLEP History of the US I (3)<br>CLEP History of the US II (3)<br>CLEP Macroeconomics (3)<br>CLEP Microeconomics (3) |
| Natural Sciences and<br>Mathematics<br>(must include 3 math and 3<br>computer science is strongly<br>recommended) | 12 | CLEP College Algebra (3)<br>CLEP Information Systems/Computers (3)<br>CLEP General Biology (6) |
| General Education Electives | 18 | CLEP Western Civilization I (3)<br>CLEP Western Civilization II (3)<br>DSST Astronomy (3)<br>DSST Human/Cultural Geography (3)<br>DSST Intro to Law Enforcement (3)<br>TECEP Science of Nutrition (3) |
| **Area of Study** | 33 | |
| American National Government | 3 | CLEP American Government (3) |
| Political Theory or Political<br>Process | 3 | TECEP Intro to Political Science (3) |
| Comparative Governments | 3 | Dual Enrollment or Community College Course<br>(3) |
| International Relations | 3 | Dual Enrollment or Community College Course<br>(3) |
| Research Methods or Statistics | 3 | DSST Principles of Statistics (3) |
| Area of Study Electives<br>(list of suggestions in the Area<br>of Study Guide Sheet) | 18 | DSST An Intro to the Modern Middle East (3)<br>DSST Rise & Fall of the Soviet Union (3)<br>DSST Environment & Humanity (3)<br>TECEP Labor Relations/Collective Bargaining (3)<br>TECEP Federal Income Taxation (3)<br>TECEP Community Health (3) |

| SAMPLE DEGREE PATH USING A B.A. IN POLITICAL SCIENCE FROM TESC (Continued) | | |
|---|---|---|
| **Subject Category** | **Credits** | **Examples of Possible Credit Sources** |
| **Free Electives** | 27 | CLEP Principles of Management (3)<br>CLEP Principles of Marketing (3)<br>DSST The Civil War & Reconstruction (3)<br>DSST Human Resource Management (3)<br>DSST Introduction to Business (3)<br>DSST Personal Finance (3)<br>DSST Technical Writing (3)<br>TECEP Database Management (3)<br>TECEP Advertising (3) |
| **Total** | **120** | |

In this example, only two actual courses would be taken; all the rest would be by CBE. What a blessing that would be for a family trying to maintain their homeschool vision all the way through. And, again, the cost should be right around $6,000 for everything!

While the above hypothetical example of a political science degree should work, there is nothing like the actual testimony of someone who has completed a course of study just recently to give us hope that it really can be done. Below is how our friend Nathanael Cordz earned a Bachelor of Science in Business Administration from TESC in only 10 months and for just under the $6,000.

The chart shows, in order, which tests he took, the number of credit hours earned, and the costs involved. At the bottom, the other costs involved in the degree are shown. You will see that the entire degree was earned using CBE's except for one online course he was required to take. The number of course requirements will vary by major depending on the availability of related CBE's, but for this degree, he only had to take one.

| BSBA IN GENERAL MANAGEMENT FROM TESC | | | |
|---|---|---|---|
| Testing Service | Examination Title | Credit Hours | Testing Fee |
| CLEP | American Government | 3 | $65 |
| CLEP | Analyzing & Interpreting Literature | 6 | $65 |
| CLEP | Introductory Sociology | 3 | $65 |
| CLEP | History of the US I | 3 | $65 |
| CLEP | Principles of Microeconomics | 3 | $65 |
| CLEP | History of the US II | 3 | $65 |
| CLEP | Principles of Macroeconomics | 3 | $65 |
| CLEP | College Mathematics | 6 | $65 |
| CLEP | Principles of Accounting | 6 | $70 |
| CLEP | Information Systems/Computer | 3 | $70 |
| CLEP | Principles of Management | 3 | $70 |
| CLEP | Principles of Marketing | 3 | $70 |
| CLEP | English Composition with Essay | 6 | $75 |
| CLEP | Introductory Business Law | 3 | $75 |
| CLEP | Natural Sciences | 6 | $70 |
| CLEP | Humanities | 6 | $70 |
| CLEP | Social Sciences & History | 6 | $75 |
| DSST | Principles of Statistics | 3 | $80 |
| DSST | Principles of Supervision | 3 | $80 |
| DSST | Organizational Behavior | 3 | $80 |
| DSST | Human Resource Management | 3 | $80 |
| DSST | Principles of Finance | 3 | $80 |
| DSST | Introduction to Business | 3 | $80 |
| DSST | Management Information Systems | 3 | $80 |
| DSST | Criminal Justice | 3 | $80 |
| TECEP | Advertising | 3 | $186 |
| TECEP | Sales Management | 3 | $186 |
| DSST | Money & Banking | 3 | $80 |
| DSST | Business Law II | 3 | $80 |
| TECEP | Business in Society | 3 | $226 |
| TECEP | Business Policy | 3 | $186 |
| CLEP | College Algebra/Trigonometry | 3 | $75 |
| | | 117 | $2,824 |
| TESC Online Course | Managerial Communications | 3 | $417 |
| | | 120 | $3,241 |

| OTHER TESC DEGREE COSTS | |
|---|---|
| Books & Other Study Material | $500 |
| CLEP Transcript Fee | $20 |
| TESC Application Fee | $75 |
| TESC Tuition | $1,880 |
| TESC Technology Services Fee | $85 |
| TESC Graduation Fee | $190 |
| Grand Total | $5,991 |

**The initial planning process**

For baccalaureate degrees, each major will consist of General Education Requirements (and maybe a separate list of core requirements for a particular degree such as business), Areas of Study Requirements, and Free Electives. The Programming Planning Handbook is your starting point and then the Areas of Study Guide Sheets fill in the rest.

We suggest the initial planning process go something like this:

1) Pick a prospective major or majors from the list earlier in this TESC section.
2) Download and print the Programming Planning Handbook from the website, and find the degree your major falls under.
3) Read the applicable General Education Requirements for that degree.
4) Download and print the Area of Study Guide Sheet for the applicable major.
5) Familiarize yourself with those requirements that will be in addition to the General Education Requirements.
6) Have the CBE lists handy from Chapter 11 of this book.
7) Compare the General Education Requirements to the CBE list and pick the CBE's you tentatively plan to take.
8) Compare the Area of Study requirements to the CBE list and pick the CBE's you tentatively plan to take.
9) Consider which CBE's you might take to satisfy your free electives.
10) If CBE's don't line up for all the requirements, consider dual enrollment, community college, online, or other resources for courses that will satisfy the leftover requisites.
11) Call TESC and ask them if you are on the right track.
12) Start taking the applicable CBE's, beginning with those with the highest pass rates.

**How does enrollment and tuition work?**

TESC's Undergraduate Prospectus goes over most of these details. It can be found on the website under Enrollment, Enrollment

Information, College Catalog, and then you will see the Undergraduate Prospectus. In addition to that document, a few hints may be warranted to help get you started.

Tuition is paid each year that the student is enrolled, so if the degree will take several years to complete, the longer you put off the enrollment process the better. However, because the enrollment is good for a year, there is no need to wait until the last minute, either. So, just start accumulating credits, enroll about a year before you plan to complete your studies, and then transfer all your credits in.

They have a Comprehensive Tuition Plan that covers the costs of taking their offered courses (as opposed to using CBE's), but most homeschoolers will likely opt for their Enrolled Options Plan because they probably will only need a course or two. By paying the Application Fee, the Annual Enrollment Tuition and the Technology Services fee, it entitles the student to a full year of service including academic advisement and program planning that is necessary because the amount of information they will give you prior to enrollment is limited.

For the 2005-2006 year, the total costs for the above are only $2,195 for a non-resident of New Jersey and $1,295 for a resident. The only other fee charged by TESC, assuming the degree would be completed within the first twelve months of enrollment, would be a graduation fee of $210. If for any reason your work is not completed within the year, additional annual tuition is $1,845.

**Does TESC require high school transcripts or ACT/SAT scores?**

The approach most homeschoolers take with TESC is to begin accumulating college credits through CBE's and dual enrollment, and then, when they have at least thirty hours and feel they are within a year of graduation, they apply to the College as a transfer student. This eliminates the need for any documentation of high school coursework, and TESC does not require ACT/SAT results from any of their prospective students.

**Is there an age requirement?**

Their literature states that a student must be 21 years old to enroll. However, if the student has accumulated at least thirty hours of college credit, they may waive that requirement. It must be requested, but everyone we know who has asked has been accepted.

Thomas Edison offers a very comprehensive variety of accredited degrees and majors and is probably our overall favorite of the Big Three, with Charter Oak being a close second. They are very easy to work with, their materials are easy to follow, and they are ready and willing to help homeschoolers achieve their academic goals.

## CHARTER OAK STATE COLLEGE
### www.cosc.edu

Charter Oak State College (COSC) was formed in 1973 within the Connecticut State System of Higher Education, just one year after Thomas Edison. Like TESC, they were established to give adult learners an alternative way to earn a degree. They take a little different approach, though. Instead of prescribing to a great extent the course of study for a particular major, they allow the student to work with his Academic Counselor to design a very personalized degree based on the student's current situation and future goals.

COSC will approve credits from the following general sources:

1) Their Own Distance Learning Courses –
   They offer both online and video courses.

2) Courses Transferred From Other Accredited Colleges and Universities –
   This could be accredited distance learning or any other classroom-based accredited work including dual enrollment.

3) Non-Collegiate Sponsored Instruction –
   Military instruction or courses evaluated by ACE may be accepted if they fit well into a COSC requirement.

4) Standardized Tests –
   CBE's are accepted and embraced as a prime source of credits.

5) Special Assessment –
   Any other course a student may have taken can be submitted to the College for consideration.

6) Contract Learning –
   A student can request approval of an independent study course overseen by a faculty mentor.

7) Portfolio Assessment –
   This option provides the student with an opportunity to demonstrate college-level knowledge obtained through experience. They make it clear that credit is not granted for "life experience," but for the learning that results from life experience.

COSC only offers four degrees: Associate in Arts, Associate in Science, Bachelor of Arts, and Bachelor of Science. The Science degrees require 50 percent of the work be in liberal arts and the Arts degrees require 75 percent liberal arts. After that, the baccalaureate student focuses on an Area of Concentration approved by the institution. He is required to submit a Concentration Plan of Study and, once approved, it becomes a learning contract.

Each degree type starts with general education requirements, includes liberal arts, an area of concentration for a B.A. or B.S., and then allows some electives. The following table summarizes the requirements by degree:

| REQUIREMENTS FOR COSC DEGREES (in credit hours) | | | | |
|---|---|---|---|---|
| Type of Requirement | Associate in Arts | Associate in Science | Bachelor of Arts | Bachelor of Science |
| **General Education Requirements** | | | | |
| Aesthetic Dimensions –<br>Examples: Art, Creative Writing, Dance, Design, Film, Literature, Music, Poetry, Theatre | 3 | 3 | 3 | 3 |
| Ethical Dimensions & Citizenship –<br>Examples: American Government, Community Organization, Introduction to Criminal Justice, Moral or Ethical Issues | 3 | 3 | 3 | 3 |
| Research –<br>Examples: Composition & Literature/Introduction to Literature, Upper Division Literature Courses, Seminars, Honors Courses, Independent Study Courses, or any Course That Requires Term Papers | 3 | 3 | 3 | 3 |
| Written Communication –<br>Subject Area: English Composition | 6 | 6 | 6 | 6 |
| Global Society –<br>Examples: Global Economics, Cultural Anthropology, International Business, and History, Literature, Politics, Religion or Cultures of Foreign Countries | 3 | 3 | 3 | 3 |
| Historical Development –<br>Art History, History, Introduction to/History of Philosophy, Music History, American Government | 3 | 3 | 3 | 3 |
| Relationship to Groups & Communities –<br>Anthropology, Human/Cultural Geography, Introduction to Communication, Introduction to Psychology, Introduction to Sociology | 3 | 3 | 3 | 3 |
| Analytical & Quantitative Reasoning & Data Interpretation –<br>Example: College-Level Mathematics | 3 | 3 | 3 | 3 |
| Scientific Process –<br>Either one 4-credit laboratory option or two 3-credit options from the following examples of natural science subjects: Astronomy, Biology, Chemistry, Ecology, Earth Science, Geology and Physics | 4-6 | 4-6 | 4-6 | 4-6 |
| Western Civilization & Culture –<br>Examples: History of Art, History, Literature or Politics of the United States or other Western Cultures | 3 | 3 | 3 | 3 |
| **General Education Totals**<br>(this number may be lower as one course or exam can satisfy more than one requirement) | **34-36** | **34-36** | **34-36** | **34-36** |
| Additional General Education from either Liberal Arts or Concentration | 0 | 0 | **4-6** | **4-6** |

| Type of Requirement (Continued) | Associate in Arts | Associate in Science | Bachelor of Arts | Bachelor of Science |
|---|---|---|---|---|
| **Area of Concentration** | 0 | 0 | 36 | 36 |
| **Elective Credits** | 24-26 | 24-26 | 44 | 44 |
| **Final Totals** (making sure a minimum of __ total hours in liberal arts) | 60 45 | 60 30 | 120 90 | 120 60 |

A full list of concentrations is listed on the next page. More detailed requirements for each one are described in COSC's Official Catalog, which can be found on their website under the Academics tab. These requirements begin on page 54 of the Catalog, with a list of which CBE's are considered liberal arts beginning on page 104.

COSC is a little different in that they are restricted on how they can describe their concentrations. They cannot be referred to as "majors." The major is in General Studies with a concentration in one of the subjects above. Concentrations that imply a professional credential, such as engineering, education or nursing, are not allowed. However, students can have concentrations in Engineering Studies, Child Studies, or Human Services/Health Studies. This approach could be a bit limiting in the marketplace, but for most areas of study, they still provide a quality Bachelor of Arts or Bachelor of Science degree, and it does offer a great deal of flexibility and creativity.

```
┌─────────────────────────────────────────────────┐
│         LIST OF COSC CONCENTRATIONS              │
├─────────────────────────────────────────────────┤
│                                                  │
│   Anthropology                                   │
│   Applied Arts                                   │
│   Applied Behavioral Science with Political Science Focus │
│   Applied Behavioral Science with Psychology Focus │
│   Applied Behavioral Science with Sociology Focus │
│   Biology                                        │
│   Business                                       │
│   Chemistry                                      │
│   Child Study                                    │
│   Communication                                  │
│   Computer Science Studies                       │
│   Criminal Justice                               │
│   Economics                                      │
│   Engineering Studies                            │
│   Fire Science Technology                        │
│   Foreign Language                               │
│   Geography                                      │
│   Health Studies                                 │
│   Health Care Administration                     │
│   History                                        │
│   Human Services Administration                  │
│   Individualized Studies                         │
│   Information Systems                            │
│   Liberal Studies                                │
│   Literature                                     │
│   Mathematics                                    │
│   Music History                                  │
│   Philosophy                                     │
│   Physics                                        │
│   Political Science                              │
│   Public Safety Administration                   │
│   Psychology                                     │
│   Religious Studies                              │
│   Sociology                                      │
│   Technology Studies                             │
│                                                  │
└─────────────────────────────────────────────────┘
```

## The initial planning process

As we did with TESC, we thought a brief suggestion of how to plan might be helpful. The planning steps could look like this:

1) Pick a prospective major and area of concentration from the list above.
2) Download and print the official COSC Official Catalog from the website and, beginning on page 44 of the 2005-06 Catalog, find your prospective area of concentration.
3) Read the applicable requirements for that concentration.

4) Have the CBE lists handy from Chapter 11 of this book.

5) Compare the General Education requirements to the CBE list and pick the CBE's you tentatively plan to take.

6) Compare the Area of Concentration requirements to the CBE list and pick the CBE's you tentatively plan to take.

7) Consider which CBE's you might take to satisfy your electives.

8) Call COSC and ask them if you are on the right track.

9) Start taking the applicable CBE's, beginning with those with the highest pass rates.

**How does enrollment and tuition work?**

The application process is very easy and is described on page 12 of the Catalog. It consists of an online or paper application, the issuing of a letter of acknowledgement from the College asking for transcripts and/or reports of prior college credits, and then the application is left open up to one year pending matriculation by the student.

Most homeschooled students will begin taking their CBE's and other non-traditional courses, but not apply until they have accumulated sixty hours. This leaves their options open before spending any money, and there is no advantage for being an enrolled student until the selected concentration needs approval. And the concentration cannot be approved until sixty hours are completed anyway.

Once the sixty hours is complete, they apply to the college at the same time they ask for approval of their area of concentration, using a Concentration Plan of Study form. They will also write an essay describing the method of study, the courses proposed to fulfill the concentration, and the reasons they are picking a particular area. COSC will then accept the course of study or suggest changes.

Costs for the 2005-06 school year include the following:

1) Application Fee of $60

2) Bachelors Matriculation Fee of $1,245 for non-Connecticut residents and $955 for Connecticut residents, which pays for an official evaluation and recording of transfer credits, faculty

review of the concentration plan, other academic advisement, records maintenance, technology, and a student association fee.

3) If the degree takes longer than one year to complete from the time of matriculation, the annual renewal fees are $630 for non-Connecticut residents and $430 for Connecticut.

4) Graduation Fee of $175

Assuming you are not a resident of the applicable home state and you achieve your degree within one year of matriculation, COSC currently costs $925 less than TESC.

**Does COSC require high school transcripts or ACT/SAT scores?**
Neither a high school transcript nor a placement test is needed. However, the student must have earned at least nine hours of college credit through any number of sources, including CBE's, to be accepted. Then, the school views the person as a transfer student and none of the traditional college incoming freshman requirements apply.

**Is there an age requirement?**
The student must be sixteen years old to apply. But your child can start collecting CBE and dual enrollment credit well before that age, in preparation for eventual enrollment.

Like Thomas Edison, Charter Oak State College is very friendly to homeschoolers, and you should not be concerned about how you will be treated. Again, the only real downside to COSC is that what most schools would consider a "major," they can only consider a "concentration." Therefore, if your child desires a more professional degree like engineering or maybe even accounting, it may limit his marketability.

## EXCELSIOR COLLEGE
**www.excelsior.edu**

Excelsior College in New York, originally called Regents College, began in 1971 "to make college degrees more accessible to busy, working adults." Focusing on what their "students knew, rather than where or how they learned it."[46]

Credit can be earned by:

1) Excelsior College Courses –
   Excelsior offers many distance courses available on CD-ROM and the web. Courses begin every two months.

2) Credit By Examination –
   As with the other two institutions, Excelsior embraces CBE's.

3) Other Distance Courses –
   Their website has links to thousands of courses from accredited colleges and universities.

4) Traditional College Courses –
   Accredited classroom-based courses are accepted, including dual enrollment.

5) Credit for Training –
   ACE-approved training is accepted by Excelsior, also.

The following degrees are offered:

---

**ECE ASSOCIATE DEGREES**

School of Business and Technology
    Business
      Associate in Science, Business
      Associate in Applied Science, Administrative/Management Studies
    Technology
      Associate in Science in Technology with Specialty
      Chemical Technologies
      Computer Technologies
      Electromagnetic Technologies
      Electronic/Instrumentation Technologies
      Manufacturing Technologies
      Mechanical/Welding Technologies
      Nuclear Technologies
      Optical Technologies
      Associate in Science in Computer Software
      Associate in Science in Electronics Technology
      Associate in Science in Nuclear Technology
      Military Specialties
      Associate in Applied Science in Aviation Studies
      Associate in Applied Science in Technical Studies (with Specialty)
      Associate in Occupational Studies in Aviation

School of Liberal Arts
    Associate in Arts
    Associate in Science

School of Nursing
    Associate in Science in Nursing
    Associate in Applied Science n Nursing

---

**ECE BACCALAUREATE DEGREES**

School of Business and Technology
    Business
      Bachelor of Science, General Business
      Bachelor of Science, Accounting
      Bachelor of Science, Finance
      Bachelor of Science, Global Business
      Bachelor of Science, Management of Human Resources
      Bachelor of Science, Marketing
      Bachelor of Science, Operations Management
      Bachelor of Science, Management Information Systems
      Bachelor of Science, Risk Management and Insurance
    Technology
      Bachelor of Science in Technology with Specialty
      Chemical Technologies
      Computer Technologies
      Electromagnetic Technologies
      Electronic/Instrumentation Technologies

**ECE BACCALAUREATE DEGREES (Continued)**

      Manufacturing Technologies
      Mechanical/Welding Technologies
      Nuclear Technologies
      Optical Technologies
      Bachelor of Science in Information Technology
      Information Security
      Network Management
      Object-Oriented Software Development
      Internet Technology for E-Commerce
      Multimedia and Web Development
      Video Game and Simulation Development
      Bachelor of Science in Computer Information Systems
      Bachelor of Science in Computer Technology
      Bachelor of Science in Electronics Engineering Technology
      Bachelor of Science in Nuclear Engineering Technology

School of Liberal Arts
    Bachelor of Arts or Bachelor of Science
    Area Studies
    Biology
    Chemistry
    Communication
    Journalism
    Rhetoric and Public Address
    Theatre
    Professional and Organizational Communication
    Radio, TV, Video and Film
    Criminal Justice
    Administration of Criminal Justice
    Corrections
    Law and Society
    Law Enforcement and Public Safety
    Economics
    Geography
    Geology
    History
    Literature in English
    Mathematics
    Music
    Philosophy
    Physics
    Political Science
    Psychology
    Sociology
    World Language and Literature

School of Nursing
    Bachelor of Science in Nursing

---

**ECE MASTER'S DEGREES**

School of Business and Technology
    Master of Business Administration

School of Liberal Arts
    Master of Arts in Liberal Studies
        Issues in Today's Society
        Global Strategies
        Educational Leadership
        Natural Science and Society
        Self-Design

School of Nursing
    Master of Science in Nursing (Clinical Systems Management)

---

## The initial planning process

We must admit that Excelsior's written materials and website are hard to navigate. They do offer a General Viewbook and then Guidelines for each major, but we could not glean nearly as much information as we found on the other two colleges.

We suggest you lay out the course requirements for a possible major, and then compare that list to the CBE lists in Chapter 11.

## How does enrollment and tuition work?

As with the other institutions, enrollment can happen at any time during a student's accumulation of credits. Earlier enrollment allows a student to take advantage of some academic advisement, but later is good because tuition renews for each year enrolled.

Baccalaureate fees include an application fee of $65, enrollment fee of $995, and a graduation fee of $495, for a total of $1,555. For students needing more than one year to complete a degree from the time of enrollment, they must pay an additional annual fee of $515.

## Does Excelsior require high school transcripts or ACT/SAT scores?

No, neither is required.

## Is there an age requirement?

We could not find one anywhere in their material.

To conclude this chapter on the Big Three, the following matrix summarizes some of the cogent points from the narrative above:

| | Thomas Edison State College | Charter Oak State College | Excelsior College |
|---|---|---|---|
| Date Founded | 1972 | 1973 | 1971 |
| State of Domicile | New Jersey | Connecticut | New York |
| Fully Accredited? | Yes | Yes | Yes |
| Types of Degrees Offered | Associates, Bachelors & Masters | Associates & Bachelors | Associates, Bachelors & Masters |
| Number of Baccalaureate Majors | 98 | 2 with 35 Concentrations | 53 |
| Written Materials Easy to Understand? | Yes, with a little orientation | Yes | Not particularly and the website is cumbersome |
| Flexibility of Course/Credit Requirements | High | Very high | High |
| Can a Degree be Achieved Almost Completely Utilizing Credit by Examination? | Yes | Yes | Yes |
| Admission Requirements | 1. High school graduate 2. 21 years of age (both requirements waived regularly if student has accrued 30 college credit hours)  Will save money if wait to enroll until less than one year away from completion | 1. 16 years of age 2. Have earned 9 hours of college credit  Will save money if wait until student has accumulated sixty hours and is ready to submit a Concentration Plan of Study | None stated  Will save money if wait to enroll until less than one year away from completion |

| (Continued) | Thomas Edison State College | Charter Oak State College | Excelsior College |
|---|---|---|---|
| High School Transcript Required? | No | No | No |
| Placement Test Such as ACT or SAT Required? | No | No | No |
| Total 2005-06 Fees Charged Assuming Out of State Tuition and Completing Coursework Within One Year of Matriculation | $2,405 | $1,480 | $1,555 |

Again, to God be the glory for giving homeschoolers a way to achieve a college degree without compromise, in an efficient manner, and with relatively little expense.

# CHAPTER 16

---

# BLENDING INDEPENDENT & TRADITIONAL APPROACHES

Throughout the book, we have been mentioning the idea that you can begin with the independent study approach and later transfer those credits to a traditional college or university in order to graduate from there. This can work well with specialized degrees or for any other reason your family may decide.

So, what are the advantages of a blended approach over a full four-year traditional degree?

1) Less Cost –
   Depending on the institution, they will normally allow several credits to be earned through CBE, dual enrollment, and other non-traditional means. For every credit earned the non-traditional way, the money you save may be your own. If a college would allow thirty hours by CBE and their tuition is $500 per credit hour, you would save approximately $14,500 on the degree. If sixty hours were acceptable, the savings would be nearly $30,000. And any dual enrollment on top of that, because those are normally accepted in addition to a college's CBE limits, reduces the tuition bill even more.

2) Less Time –
Because CBE credits can be earned so much faster than a traditional classroom course, there is less wasted time. That time saved could be devoted to other things or to accelerating the program.

3) Starting Early –
If a student starts in high school, and the college they are considering will accept several non-traditional credits, there is no reason the student couldn't be a college junior, or at least a sophomore, by the time he hits traditional college age.

4) Skip the Compromising General Education Courses –
It is the general education courses that concern our family the most with regard to compromising professors or course content. If you are majoring in business, you probably won't find much negative influence in the upper grades, but you would still have to take psychology, a science, philosophy, etc. on campus. If those credits can be knocked out by CBE, in a hurry, and without the influence of a potentially harmful professor, all the better.

5) Skip Earlier Courses Where the Folly is Likely the Highest –
We think it is safe to say that college freshmen are wilder than juniors and seniors. As a result, finishing a degree at a brick-and-mortar campus is probably less compromising than starting one there.

6) Allows a Student to Enter Traditional College as a Transfer Student Rather Than an Incoming Freshman –
This is one of the greatest advantages of this approach and a real secret weapon for homeschoolers. If you want your child to earn a degree from a traditional college, and you were worried about how he would get in, taking several CBE's and dual enrollment will negate all those fears. Your child will go

in as a transfer student, so the need for high school transcripts and placement tests usually disappears.

Next, what are the disadvantages of a blended approach versus a full independent study degree?

1) More Cost –
   The inverse is true of the above. If the last two or three years is at a traditional college, versus one of the Big Three, full tuition will be paid during those years. Given the example above of $500 per credit hour and the last three years at a regular college (even at a local college and thereby avoiding room and board), the student will be paying nearly $45,000 more than with a fully independent degree.

2) More Time –
   The inverse of the above is also true here.

3) May Still Have Compromising Coursework and Professors –
   Even though the higher grades are probably less dangerous, the possibility always exists that people will try to "take you captive by philosophy and empty deceit, according to human tradition, according to the elemental spirits of the world, and not according to Christ" (Colossians 2:8). The independent study approach is just plain safer.

4) Non-Traditional Credit Accumulation Will Be Limited –
   Traditional higher education institutions vary greatly on the number of non-traditional credits they are willing to accept, but they all cut you off somewhere. "Select" schools, like those in the Ivy League and other similarly esteemed institutions, tend not to accept any independent study credits. Others may take up to sixty hours. Thirty to forty five seems to be a general rule for the run of the mill local college. The bottom

line is that the hungrier the school is, the more non-traditional credits they will take. Select schools can afford to have firmer rules, because they have several other students lined up who will spend all their money there.

With all that being said, the blended approach can be a wonderful tool for homeschoolers. It allows us to chisel away a significant number of course requirements before our children are college age. If we focus on attaining as many CBE's as a potential campus will allow, and then add dual enrollment on top of that, we will present strong and proven student records acceptable to almost any prospective admissions department. With enough hours earned, we can show a strong, college-level transcript instead of a homeschool high school document we created. We also give our children the gift of a shortened course to their college graduation, as well as a substantial savings for their future.

This blended method, then, may be a good choice for some students who want to start early and save some money, but who desire a degree from a traditional institution. This could be because they are looking for a degree not offered by the Big Three, or just because they see the benefit of having live professors for the courses in their major. These are all decisions best left to an individual family, but we hope we have given you some things to think about in the process.

# CHAPTER 17

---

## SOME OTHER PRACTICAL THINGS WE'VE LEARNED

We had a few other things to pass on, but they didn't fit neatly into one of the other chapters. So, we thought we would list here, in no particular order, some of the miscellaneous information we've learned so far along the way:

1) www.degreeinfo.com –
   We have found this website to be very helpful. It contains an online Discussion Board where students looking for the best ways to achieve distance and independent study degrees can post their questions, successes and failures. It is visited mostly by adult learners who have been out of the formal higher education environment for some time and are wise enough to be better consumers of education. We have never posted anything, but have spent time reading others' advice. The Big Three also monitor the site and often give direct answers to questions.

2) www.123collegedegree.com –
   This website offers helpful explanations on how to get a degree from one of the Big Three. It also offers tips on how to study for the CBE tests, and even gives their suggestions for textbooks. They promote InstantCert (www.instantcert.com)

and a series of study guides from www.istudysmart.com. We explored InstantCert in Chapter 12, and we like them a lot. The iStudySmart study guides, however, run between $170 and $200, and you still need to purchase a textbook. They are available online, on CD-ROM, and on paper.

3) You Can Find Many Books on Amazon or eBay –
There are many textbooks and test prep guides available out in cyberspace. You may want to check there first. You also can resell them on the internet when you no longer need them.

4) Calling Out CBE Credits –
We suggest you hold all credits at the CBE testing services until such time as they are needed. There really is no reason to send them to a college before the child enrolls at the institution where they plan to graduate. And if you call them out as you need them, they cannot affect any status you may want later. For instance, scholarships sometimes are only available to freshmen, so if you are doing the blended approach, you may be able to still get a scholarship and then later call out your CBE's. You may want to call out just enough to go in as a transfer student, avoiding a high school transcript and the ACT or SAT, but still protecting your scholarship potential. The idea, for blended approach students, is to read a prospective college's handbook carefully and call out your CBE's in the manner that gives you the best advantage.

5) Scholarship Qualification Requires Full-Time Status –
This is just something to keep in mind if your student is using the blended approach. Part-time students normally are not eligible for scholarships. However, there are many other advantages to going part time, especially if many credits have been earned while still in high school and the student has other things going on in their life.

6) What to Do If Your Blended-Approach College Charges Too Much for CBE Transfers –

As has been stated previously, some schools charge their regular credit hour tuition to accept CBE's, some others may charge their dual enrollment rate, while most only charge a nominal fee. Regardless, if the school you want to graduate from has a hefty fee, you may be able to transfer your CBE's first to an institution with a nominal fee, and then later transfer them from that college to yours. We've heard this can sometimes avoid the charge, but you will probably want to ask some questions first.

7) CLEP English Composition Tests –

Many schools that you may be interested in, for the blended approach, do not accept CLEP Composition exams. This subject, almost universally required to graduate, may best be earned through dual enrollment. We haven't tried it yet, but we plan on letting our next child try out Liberty University's online dual enrollment for Comp I and Comp II. We've heard good things about it.

8) Analyzing and Interpreting Literature CLEP –

This CLEP test is a bit of a secret weapon for homeschoolers. It provides six hours of credit with very little preparation. The test consists of reading passages of literature and answering questions about what was read. There is no prior knowledge of literature necessary. The child should start by taking the practice test in the CLEP Official Study Guide, and if he does well, he is ready to take the exam (remember to grade the test for your child, so he can take it again later if needed). If more practice is needed, our children will review some literature passages and questions in an ACT or SAT practice book or look over the REA test prep guide on the subject. This CLEP usually satisfies an English and/or Humanities requirement.

9) College Algebra CLEP –

   The College Algebra CLEP exam is basically high school Algebra I and II. So, when a homeschool high school student finishes Algebra II (by the way, Saxon has worked wonderfully for this purpose), they should go take the CLEP exam. They probably will still want to take the practice test in the CLEP Official Study Guide first to make sure they are ready, but the important thing is to take the exam right away before the information is forgotten. That way, if they enter college using a blended approach, they will not need to sit for a math placement test and risk having to take a remedial class.

10) College Course Admissions Placement –

   Often colleges have testing requirements, as part of their admissions process, in order to place a student in the correct level of their general education classes. Some of the families in our store, interested in the blended approach, have gotten around having to take these tests by passing some targeted CBE's or dual enrollment classes in advance. The ones to take would be dual enrolled College Comp I and II to satisfy the language arts placement test, Analyzing and Interpreting Literature CLEP to satisfy the reading portion, and then, as mentioned above, College Algebra CLEP to satisfy math. These should demonstrate to the college that proficiency has already been attained.

11) Where to Send DANTES Exams –

   Unlike CLEP, DANTES requires you to list a university that should receive the results, in addition to the results they will send to you. We simply asked the university where our child took the exam for their code number, and they were more than happy to give it even though our child was not enrolled. We still received the results at our house, and it was a way to satisfy their policy.

12) DANTES Speech Exam –

Although we haven't done it ourselves, we keep hearing that the DANTES Speech exam is an easy pass. After looking over a speech textbook, and preparing to answer the multiple choice questions on the test, you will prepare to give a speech into a microphone at the testing center. We understand that making the speech the proper length of time is one of the most important things, and that they are very lenient on the content. The military pass rate for this exam is 85 percent.

13) Two-Year to Four-Year Degrees –

When transferring an entire Associate's degree into a four-year institution, they normally are very friendly about taking all sixty hours. When an Associates is not complete, they may pick and choose which courses will transfer. Also, we have seen some of our customers go the Associates route first in order to avoid a large amount of general education requirements, because those tend to be the most impure. Associate's degrees normally require only a few gen ed classes. The entire Associates is transferred in, and the student can usually fill what would have been gen ed with electives of their choice. If you are not able to find a school that will let you skip the gen ed's, you might look into an adult evening and weekend program, which usually is more accommodating.

14) Pre-Requisite Requirements Vary By School –

Some colleges require a very specific order to the classes you take. Others are softer. If your child wants to take Chemistry, for example, some schools may demand two or three pre-req's before allowing the child to take that course. Others may not care. The flexible school could be more desirable if your student is using the blended approach and going part-time, because they are piecing together courses outside the regular rhythm of a full-time student.

15) Foreign Language Much Less Required Today –
Many of us who went to college years ago would remember that foreign language was required for many majors. This is just not the case anymore, although you should always check. Some colleges may still want to see it on a high school transcript, but since we are advocating going in as a transfer student, it applies even less.

In concluding this section on the tools, we thought we should take a moment to debunk the notion that you get what you pay for in an education. In other words, the amount of money spent on college does not equal the value. The quality of an education flows from the efforts of the student.

It may seem at times that we are suggesting shortcuts. I guess we are for the "yikes!" courses, but for everything else, the student should learn the subject well. You are simply sticking with the independent study and/or tutor approach you have embraced through your previous homeschool years.

And don't forget that textbook education is only a small piece of a young person's training. As we know well, the discipleship of our children in the fear and admonition of the Lord is what really counts. The other approach is to send them off for a very formal and expensive "education," when most of what they are getting is just indoctrination into the world.

So don't ever apologize, or feel inferior, for taking what we believe to be this "wise" way. I (Scott) told our story to an acquaintance recently that had just sent his daughter off to a northeast college for four years. He actually wasn't very happy with me for telling him, because at that point he really didn't want to know there was a better, and much less expensive, way.

We hope you are feeling confident and ready to set your course!

# SECTION V

---

# MULTIGENERATIONAL FAITHFULNESS

# CHAPTER 18

---

# RESETTING
# WHAT'S NORMAL

Our family loves the phrase "multigenerational faithfulness." We heard it first from Doug Phillips a few years ago and were amazed by the transforming power of that phrase alone. It is what our families need. It is what our churches need. It is what our nation needs.

We have become such an individualistic society that focuses so much on self, instead of on those great treasures we tuck into bed each night. We are called to pass down to our children our knowledge and devotion to the Creator, so they can teach their children, so they can teach *their* children, and so on. This is a central message of the Scriptures.

Stewart Jordan is a pastor from the Huntsville, Alabama area that we have come to know and love. He wrote a wonderful paper on the church and home called "Catching God's Heart and Design." In it he states:

*Ministry is to be pursued both in an outward way in our generation and in a downward way in the generations to come.*[47]

Regrettably, much of the church has adopted the self-focused philosophies of the world, which lead us to live life our own way. We would rather feed our own flesh than nurture and train our children.

In *When You Rise Up*, R.C. Sproul, Jr. writes:

*God begins with the dominion mandate, to exercise dominion over the creation. And since God doesn't change, that ultimate goal abides. The goal is restated in Ecclesiastes – the sum of the matter is this: to fear God and obey whatsoever He commands (Ecclesiastes 12:13). And then Jesus reiterates the same theme in a slightly different key when He tells us that we ought to seek first the Kingdom of God, and His righteousness. Our children are made to seek God, as we are. Therefore, if we are to train our children rightly, we must expunge from our own hearts that overarching agenda of the culture around us, the pursuit of personal peace and affluence.[48]*

Our culture, including the modern evangelical church, does not really care about children. We can't wait to abdicate our responsibilities to anyone who will take them. Day care leads to preschool. Preschool leads to school. School leads to intense peer dependence. And peer dependence leads to a deafening lack of interest in the things of God.

On the other hand, true family nurture and discipleship leads to a dependence first on parents and then on the Savior whom the parents long to please and serve. Our children should be raised by parents with the help of the church, not by the state with the help of the church. Because when the state rocks the cradle, the church will be nothing more than a religious-sounding extension of the culture.

When our eyes were first opened to this idea of a multigenerational vision, the Bible suddenly took on a different flavor. If you have ever changed theological perspectives, you know that when you read the Word with a new framework, never before understood passages become clear, and others can be placed in proper context. We won't take the time to completely defend the Biblical basis for multigenerational thinking, but a few thoughts are warranted:

1) In the first suggestion of a gospel message in the Scriptures, God promises, after the Fall, to put enmity between the serpent's *offspring* and the woman's *offspring* (Genesis 3:15).

2) In the law given to Moses, the phrase "throughout your generations" is used thirty eight times.

3) Each of the major covenants in the Bible use terminology such as "for all future generations" (Noahic Covenant in Genesis 9:12), "you and your offspring after you throughout their generations" (Abrahamic Covenant in Genesis 17:7), and "establish your offspring forever, and build your throne for all generations" (Davidic Covenant in Psalm 89:4).

4) At the dawn of the New Covenant, it was declared that "he will turn the hearts of fathers to their children and the hearts of children to their fathers" (Malachi 4:6).

5) On training for the benefit of future generations, the Scriptures teach: "that he may command his children and his household after him" (Genesis 18:19), "teach them diligently to your children" (Deuteronomy 6:7), "proclaim your might to another generation" (Psalm 71:18), "that the next generation might know them, the children yet unborn, and arise and tell them to their children" (Psalm 78:6), "one generation shall commend your works to another" (Psalm 145:4), "tell your children of it, and let your children tell their children, and their children to another generation" (Joel 1:3), and "bring them up in the discipline and instruction of the Lord" (Ephesians 6:4).

The Bible screams out for us to love and train our children for the glory of God and for the good of the generations that will follow. We are not just training our children, but also our great, great, great grandchildren.

Psalm 78 begins:

*A Maskil of Asaph. Give ear, O my people, to my teaching; incline your ears to the words of my mouth! I will open my mouth in a parable; I will utter dark sayings from of old, things that we have heard and known, that our fathers have told us. We will not hide them from their children, but tell to the coming generation the glorious deeds of the Lord, and his might, and the wonders that he has done. He established a testimony in Jacob and appointed a law in Israel, which he commanded our fathers to teach to their children, that the next generation might know them, the children yet unborn, and arise and tell them to their children, so that they should set their hope in God and not forget the works of God, but keep his commandments; and that they should not be like their fathers, a stubborn and rebellious generation, a generation whose heart was not steadfast, whose spirit was not faithful to God. (Psalm 78:1-8)*

To summarize, this passage instructs us to listen to the words that God has given to our fathers, then to tell the next generation about His glorious deeds, might and wonders. Then, those children would pass it to the next generation, and so on. So that they should set their hope in God and not forget His great works, but remain steadfast.

It's all about our children not forgetting! And the only way they will not forget is if we keep telling them. If the culture of our home is one of teaching them diligently and talking of the wonderful works of God "when you sit in your house, and when you walk by the way, and when you lie down, and when you rise" (Deuteronomy 6:7), how could they possibly forget? And if they do not forget, they will keep His commandments and pass this beautiful, biblical vision down to their children. This is how it is supposed to work!

It doesn't mean you always have the Bible open as you go about your day, but it does mean you are consistently reminding your children about His hand upon this earth and in their lives. And God's might and gracious works do not end with the closing of the Canon. They also need to be reminded of His hand in history over the last two thousand years and His providence in your own family. There are great stories of power, grace and redemption all around us, and we should take the opportunity to talk of these things.

There is a beautiful family in our church, the Ritters, who have adopted eighteen children from many different backgrounds. As you can imagine, their family history is full of glorious stories of redemption and God's loving kindness. The Exodus would not have been as wonderful were it not for the time of slavery. And like God's might shown in the parting of the waters, His power is no less dramatic as He turns hearts of stone to hearts of flesh and "turn[s] the hearts of fathers to their children and the hearts of children to their fathers" (Malachi 4:6).

The good fruit that results from embracing this multigenerational view can be astounding. Jonathan and Sarah Edwards' ancestral line is a stark contrast to that of a contemporary of his day. The following was taken from an Edwards biography:

*In 1900, A.E. Winship tracked down fourteen hundred of their descendants and published a study of the Edwards children in contrast to the Jukes family, the notorious clan who cost New York State a total of $1,250,000 in welfare and custodial charges. Jukes wasn't actually the name of the other family. The word means "to roost," and it was used about them because the family were social floaters, with no home or nest. They all originated with one immigrant who settled in upstate New York in 1720 and produced a tribe of "idleness, ignorance, and vulgarity."*

*Only 20 of the 1,200 Jukes had ever had gainful employment (the others were criminals or lived on state aid), whereas the Edwards family had contributed astonishing riches to the American scene. "Whatever the family has done it has done ably and nobly," Winship contended.*

*By 1900 when Winship made his study, this single marriage had produced 13 college presidents, 65 professors, 100 lawyers and a dean of an outstanding law school, 30 judges, 60 physicians and a dean of a medical school, and 80 holders of public office including three United States Senators, mayors of three large cities, governors of three states, a Vice President of the United States and a controller of the United States Treasury.*

*Members of the family wrote 135 books... They edited eighteen journals and periodicals. They entered the ministry in platoons and sent one hundred missionaries overseas... As Winship put it... "The family has cost the country nothing in pauperism, in crime, in hospital or asylum service; on the contrary it represents the highest usefulness."*

*The line continues to be vigorous, intelligent, enlivening to society. Yet all this achievement came out of a family with no large inherited fortune. All the children's accomplishments were the result of their personal initiative.*[49]

Given the title of this chapter, let us contemplate what normal should be for our children. We talk about normalness, or the culture of the home, because the environment we create for our children now is more than likely what they will take with them into their future families. The more we can model godly behavior, the easier it will be for our children to progress beyond our failings. If normal is the pursuit of godliness and serving others, our children will have the privilege of starting from that point.

We know so many first-generation Christians attempting to walk this narrow path without much guidance from their past, but God is most definitely doing a work in our time! And we believe in "generationally-progressive sanctification." We think it is our job as parents to put off as much of the old self as we can, put on the new, and then pass down just the new. Then, as the generations unfold, our descendants, as well as the bride of Christ, will become ever more pure and lovely to the Bridegroom.

We believe the normalness we all should be striving for is in the "ancient paths" that were lost during Jeremiah's day and are lost again today.

> *Thus says the Lord: "Stand by the roads, and look, and ask for the ancient paths, where the good way is; and walk in it, and find rest for your souls." (Jeremiah 6:16a)*

This does not mean we need to be old-fashioned in everything we do. There is a lot to be learned from some good, old-fashioned ways, but that is not the point here. God has us placed in our time and culture for a reason. The ancient paths spoken of in Jeremiah are God's ways. They are a reminder of His faithfulness to His people and love for His bride.

Matthew Henry, a wonderful eighteenth-century commentator, further clarifies this passage:

> *We must not be guided merely by antiquity, as if the plea of prescription and long usage were alone sufficient to justify our path. No; there is an old way which wicked men have trodden (Job 22:15). But, when we ask for the old paths, it is only in order to find out the good way, the highway of the upright.*[50]

Let's also not forget that we need to be about the Lord's business and to be taking dominion over the earth. And taking dominion is not a single generation proposition. It requires multiple generations to accomplish. But if we: 1) can be fruitful and multiply, 2) pass down the wonderful works of God to the next generation so that they will not forget, and 3) become more and more sanctified as the generations progress, we will be fulfilling our calling to bring the earth under His purposes. The world changes as the church changes, for better or for worse.

The normalness we are striving to pass down is this multigenerational vision, a love for God, a love for His church, a love and care for children, a love and care for those in need, and the desire to be a sweet fragrance to a lost and dying world. We can either pack our children's bags with these glorious gifts or hand them a variety of handicaps to overcome.

How does this all relate to higher education? As homeschoolers, our children are being raised differently, and we can't give up so close to the finish line. Take them all the way through, and only send them off purposefully, and only when they are truly ready. Be careful about just parking them at college for four years where they will likely be exposed to many things you have strived to protect them from during their first eighteen years.

Think also about courtship. If you have embraced this model for your family, how could you possibly make that happen when they are hundreds of miles from home? Even if they did not succumb to temptation, it would be extremely impractical to make the process work long distance.

So, while much of the rest of the world's parents are needlessly spending their hard-earned money, or their children are amassing huge amounts of debt and putting their lives on hold for four years, we can take back our children's education. As homeschoolers, we have already taken back that education in the earlier years, and we pray that this book has presented the how-to's clearly enough to help you finish it in the same manner.

This independent study method has been life changing for us, and we hope it will be for you also. In previous chapters, we have outlined many of the blessings of going this route, but for our family the greatest difference it brought was giving all of us a brand new outlook on our educational life. We had always dreaded the thought of traditional college for our children, not to mention that we had no idea how we were going to pay for it!

A great deal of our home life now is spent talking through their futures. The older children have also been a great encouragement to each other as they help one another discern their gifts and interests and the best path to further their academic training. In other words, it gives our family one more common bond to rally around, and our young men and women would tell you that they feel very loved in and through the process.

And while we're talking about resetting what is normal in our homes, make sure it is all sweetened with an inexpressible joy.

*These things I have spoken to you, that my joy may be in you, and that your joy may be full. (John 15:11)*

These are the last years with your children, and if you can send them off into their adult lives with a deep and abundant joy, what a blessing that would be. Make these final times at home fun and sweet and vibrant. Make them full of serving the saints and neighbors. Make them full of talking about their future homes and families. By doing so, you will be making all these things normal and they, in turn, will teach their children, who will then never forget the wonderful works of God!

As we have stated many times, academics is only one piece of the child-rearing puzzle. The main goal is to send them out strong, prepared to love and serve their Lord. We believe this independent study method of attaining a college education will enhance, rather than detract from, this end.

But because higher education is not the end, only a potential means, college will not be necessary to fulfill every young person's individual vision. The last thing we would want this book to do is to make anyone feel that college is somehow a higher calling or is a necessary part of every Christian's training. In fact, for many, it would slow them down in their pursuits. However, if you feel college is either right or necessary, this method should help you reach that goal in a much more practical and protected way.

So, in final conclusion, if you believe a higher education is in God's will for one or more of your children, we pray this vision about college can help protect and fulfill what you have already begun with the rest of your family's life and purpose. We hope that the idea of starting early is invigorating, that the suggestion of an accelerated and inexpensive degree is encouraging, and that you are freed by the thought of knowing the purity you have strived to protect will not be compromised.

Blessings to you and your family as you seek God's ways!

*Praise the Lord! Blessed is the man who fears the Lord, who greatly delights in his commandments! His offspring will be mighty in the land; the generation of the upright will be blessed. (Psalm 112:1-2)*

# APPENDIX

# "A Father's Resolutions"

You might wonder, especially earlier in the book, why we quote so much from men of the past. The answer lies in our belief that God has been working through His people throughout history, and it is always encouraging to see others' victories, insights, and even struggles, as they have pressed ever-forward to take dominion and grow God's Kingdom here on earth. It is very inspiring to see how they have fought against the enemies of the day, and have tried to elevate our Lord to His rightful place in the Church, and hopefully even in the culture. We do ourselves, and those around us, a great disservice to think that God's illumination is only for our time. His redemptive history marches on, and a love for, and study of, its unfolding is a worthwhile pursuit.

Charles Spurgeon once said, in speaking about the reading of Bible commentators of the past:

> It seems odd, that certain men who talk so much of what the Holy Spirit reveals to themselves, should think so little of what he has revealed to others. You must be content to learn of holy men, taught of God, and mighty in the Scriptures. A respectable acquaintance with the opinions of the giants of the past, might have saved many an erratic thinker from wild interpretations and outrageous inferences.[51]

Understanding the thinking of those who have gone before us helps protect the Church from making the same mistakes over and over. The particular men's words used in this book, we believe, are especially helpful as they show that the remnant's commitment to multigenerational faithfulness is not new. And much can be learned from their devotion to its cause.

All that being said, we thought it would be an encouragement to pass on the following list of Resolutions, penned by Cotton Mather three hundred years ago and quoted several times earlier in the book. They are a great example of the mighty work of the Church and an encouragement still today to hold tightly and dearly to those beautiful arrows in our quiver.

# A FATHER'S RESOLUTIONS

By Cotton Mather, Puritan Pastor (1663-1728)
Massachusetts Bay Colony, Boston

PARENTS, Oh! how much ought you to be continually devising for the good of your *children!* Often device how to make them "wise children"; how to give them a desirable education, an education that may render them desirable; how to render them lovely and polite, and serviceable in their generation. Often devise how to enrich their minds with valuable knowledge; how to instill generous, gracious, and heavenly principles into their minds; how to restrain and rescue them from the paths of the destroyer, and fortify them against their peculiar temptations. There is a world of good that you have to do for them. You are without the natural feelings of humanity if you are not in a continual agony to do for them all the good that ever you can. It was no mistake of an ancient writer to say, "Nature teaches us to love our children as ourselves."

RESOLVED —

1. At the birth of my children, I will resolve to do all I can that they may be the Lord's. I will now actually give them up by faith to God; entreating that each child may be a child of God the Father, a subject of God the Son, a temple of God the Spirit — and be rescued from the condition of a child of wrath, and be possessed and employed by the Lord as an everlasting instrument of His glory.

2. As soon as my children are capable of minding my admonitions, I will often, often admonish them, saying, "Child, God has sent His son to die, to save sinners from death and hell. You must not sin against Him. You must every day cry to God that He would be your Father, and your Saviour, and your Leader. You must

renounce the service of Satan, you must not follow the vanities of this world, you must lead a life of serious religion.

3. Let me daily pray for my children with constancy, with fervency, with agony. Yea, by name let me mention each one of them every day before the Lord. I will importunately beg for all suitable blessings to be bestowed upon them: that God would give them grace, and give them glory, and withhold no good thing from them; that God would smile on their education, and give His good angels the charge over them, and keep them from evil, that it may not grieve them; that when their father and mother shall forsake them, the Lord may take them up. With importunity I will plead that promise on their behalf: "The Heavenly Father will give the Holy Spirit unto them that ask Him." Oh! happy children, if by asking I may obtain the Holy Spirit for them!

4. I will early entertain the children with delightful stories out of the Bible. In the talk of the table, I will go through the Bible, when the olive-plants about my table are capable of being so watered. But I will always conclude the stories with some lessons of piety to be inferred from them.

5. I will single out some Scriptural sentences of the greatest importance; and some also that have special antidotes in them against the common errors and vices of children. They shall quickly get those golden sayings by heart, and be rewarded with silver or gold, or some good thing, when they do it. Such as,
   - Psalm 11:10—"The fear of the Lord is the beginning of wisdom."
   - Matthew 16:26—"What is a man profited, if he shall gain the whole world, and lose his own soul?"
   - 1 Timothy 1:15—"Christ Jesus came into the world to save sinners; of whom I am chief."

- Matthew 6:6—"When thou prayest, enter into thy closet, and when thou hast shut thy door, pray to thy Father which is in secret."
- Ephesians 4:25—"Putting away lying, speak every man truth with his neighbour."
- Romans 12:17, 19—"Recompense to no man evil for evil... Dearly beloved, avenge not yourselves."

6. Jewish treatise tells us that among the Jews, when a child began to speak, the father was bound to teach him Deuteronomy 33:4—"Moses commanded us a law, even the inheritance of the congregation of Jacob." Oh! let me early make my children acquainted with the Law which our blessed Jesus has commanded us! 'Tis the best inheritance I can give them.

7. I will cause my children to learn the Catechism. In catechizing them, I will break the answers into many lesser and proper questions; and by their answer to them, observe and quicken their understandings. I will bring every truth into some duty and practice, and expect them to confess it, and consent unto it, and resolve upon it. As we go on in our catechizing, they shall, when they are able, turn to the proofs and read them, and say to me what they prove and how. Then, I will take my times, to put nicer and harder questions to them; and improve the times of conversation with my family (which every man ordinarily has or may have) for conferences on matters of religion.

8. Restless will I be till I may be able to say of my children, "Behold, they pray!" I will therefore teach them to pray. But after they have learnt a form of prayer, I will press them to proceed unto points that are not in their form. I will charge them with all possible cogency to pray in secret; and often call upon them, "Child, I hope, you don't forget my charge to you, about secret prayer: your crime is very great if you do!"

9. I will do what I can very early to beget a temper of kindness in my children, both toward one another and toward all other people. I will instruct them how ready they should be to share with others a part of what they have; and they shall see my encouragements when they discover a loving, a courteous, an helpful disposition. I will give them now and then a piece of money, so that with their own little hands they may dispense unto the poor. Yea, if any one has hurt them, or vexed them, I will not only forbid them all revenge, but also oblige them to do a kindness as soon as may be to the vexatious person. All coarseness of language or carriage in them, I will discountenance.

10. I will be solicitous to have my children expert, not only at reading handsomely, but also at writing a fair hand. I will then assign them such books to read as I may judge most agreeable and profitable; obliging them to give me some account of what they read; but keep a strict eye upon them, that they don't stumble on the Devil's library, and poison themselves with foolish romances, or novels, or plays, or songs, or jests that are not convenient. I will set them also, to write out such things as may be of the greatest benefit unto them; and they shall have their blank books, neatly kept on purpose, to enter such passages as I advise them to. I will particularly require them now and then to write a prayer of their own composing, and bring it unto me; that so I may discern what sense they have of their own everlasting interests.

11. I wish that my children may as soon as may be, feel the principles of reason and honor working in them—and that I may carry on their education, very much upon those principles. Therefore, first, I will wholly avoid that harsh, fierce, crabbed usage of the children that would make them tremble and abhor to come into my presence. I will treat them so that they shall fear to offend me, and yet mightily love to see me, and be glad of my coming home if I have been abroad at any time. I will have it looked upon as a severe and awful punishment to be forbidden for awhile to come

into my presence. I will raise in them an high opinion of their father's love to them, and of his being better able to judge what is good for them than they are for themselves. I will bring them to believe 'tis best for them to be and do as I will have them. Hereupon I will continually magnify the matter to them, what a brave thing 'tis to know the things that are excellent; and more brave to do the things that are virtuous. I will have them to propose it as a reward of their well-doing at any time, I will now go to my father, and he will teach me something that I was never taught before. I will have them afraid of doing any base thing, from an horror of the baseness in it. My first response to finding a lesser fault in them shall be a surprise, a wonder, vehemently expressed before them, that ever they should be guilty of doing so foolishly; a vehement belief that they will never do the like again; a weeping resolution in them, that they will not. I will never dispense a blow, except it be for an atrocious crime or for a lesser fault obstinately persisted in; either for an enormity, or for an obstinacy. I will always proportion the chastisements to the miscarriages; neither smiting bitterly for a very small piece of childishness nor frowning only a little for some real wickedness. Nor shall my chastisement ever be dispensed in a passion and a fury; but I will first show them the command of God, by transgressing whereof they have displeased me. The slavish, raving, fighting way of discipline is too commonly used. I look upon it as a considerable article in the wrath and curse of God upon a miserable world.

12. As soon as we can, we'll get up to yet higher principles. I will often tell the children what cause they have to love a glorious Christ, who has died for them. And how much He will be well-pleased with their well-doing. And what a noble thing 'tis to follow His example; which example I will describe unto them. I will often tell them that the eye of God is upon them; the great God knows all they do and hears all they speak. I will often tell them that there will be a time when they must appear before the Judgment-Seat of

the holy Lord; and they must now do nothing that may then be a grief and shame unto them. I will set before them the delights of that Heaven that is prepared for pious children; and the torments of that Hell that is prepared of old for naughty ones. I will inform them of the good things the good angels do for little ones that have the fear of God and are afraid of sin. And how the devils tempt them to do ill things; how they hearken to the devils, and are like them, when they do such things; and what mischiefs the devils may get leave to do them in this world, and what a sad thing 'twill be, to be among the devils in the Place of Dragons. I will cry to God, that He will make them feel the power of these principles.

13. When the children are of a fit age for it, I will sometimes closet them; have them with me alone; talk with them about the state of their souls; their experiences, their proficiencies, their temptations; obtain their declared consent unto every jot and tittle of the gospel; and then pray with them, and weep unto the Lord for His grace, to be bestowed upon them, and make them witnesses of the agony with which I am travailing to see the image of Christ formed in them. Certainly, they'll never forget such actions!

14. I will be very watchful and cautious about the companions of my children. I will be very inquisitive what company they keep; if they are in hazard of being ensnared by any vicious company, I will earnestly pull them out of it, as brands out of the burning. I will find out, and procure, laudable companions for them.

15. As in catechizing the children, so in the repetition of the public sermons, I will use this method. I will put every truth into a question to be answered with Yes or No. By this method I hope to awaken their attention as well as enlighten their understanding. And thus I shall have an opportunity to ask, "Do you desire such or such a grace of God?" and the like. Yea, I may have opportunity to demand, and perhaps to obtain their early and frequent (and why not sincere?) consent unto the glorious gospel. The Spirit of

Grace may fall upon them in this action; and they may be seized by Him, and held as His temples, through eternal ages.

16. When a Day of Humiliation arrives, I will make them know the meaning of the day. And after time given them to consider of it, I will order them to tell me what special afflictions they have met with, and what good they hope to get by those afflictions. On a Day of Thanksgiving, they shall also be made to know the intent of the Day. And after consideration, they shall tell me what mercies of God unto them they take special notice of, and what duties to God they confess and resolve under such obligations. Indeed, for something of this importance, to be pursued in my conversation with the children, I will not confine myself unto the solemn days, which may occur too seldom for it. Very particularly, on the birthdays of the children, I will take them aside, and mind them of the age which (by God's grace) they are come unto; how thankful they should be for the mercies of God which they have hitherto lived upon; how fruitful they should be in all goodness, that so they may still enjoy their mercies. And I will inquire of them whether they have ever yet begun to mind the work which God sent them into the world upon; how far they understand the work; and what good strokes they have struck at it; and, how they design to spend the rest of their time, if God still continue them in the world.

17. When the children are in any trouble—if they be sick, or pained—I will take advantage therefrom, to set before them the evil of sin, which brings all our trouble; and how fearful a thing it will be to be cast among the damned, who are in ceaseless and endless trouble. I will set before them the benefit of an interest in a CHRIST, by which their trouble will be sanctified unto them, and they will be prepared for death, and for fullness of joy in a happy eternity after death.

18. Among all the points of education which I will endeavor for my children, I hope to see that each of them—the daughters as well as the sons—may gain insight into some skill that lies in the way of gain (however their own inclination may most carry them), so that they may be able to subsist themselves, and get something of a livelihood, in case the Providence of God should bring them into necessities. Why not they as well as Paul the Tent-Maker! The children of the best fashion, may have occasion to bless the parents that make such a provision for them! The Jews have a saying worth remembering: "Whoever doesn't teach his son some trade or business, teaches him to be a thief."

19. As soon as ever I can, I will make my children apprehensive of the main end for which they are to live; that so they may as soon as may be, begin to live; and their youth not be nothing but vanity. I will show them, that their main end must be, to, acknowledge the great God, and His glorious Christ; and bring others to acknowledge Him: and that they are never wise nor well, but when they are doing so. I will make them able to answer the grand question of why they live; and what is the end of the actions that fill their lives? I will teach them that their Creator and Redeemer is to be obeyed in everything, and everything is to be done in obedience to Him. I will teach them how even their diversions, and their ornaments, and the tasks of their education, must all be to fit them for the further service of Him to whom I have devoted them; and how in these also, His commandments must be the rule of all they do. I will sometimes therefore surprise them with an inquiry, "Child, what is this for? Give me a good account of why you do it?" How comfortably shall I see them walking in the light, if I may bring them wisely to answer this inquiry.

20. I will oblige the children to retire sometimes, and ponder on that question: "What shall I wish to have done, if I were now a-dying?"—and report unto me their own answer to the question; of

186

which I will then take advantage, to inculcate the lessons of godliness upon them.

21. If I live to see the children marriageable, I will, before I consult with Heaven and earth for their best accommodation in the married state, endeavor the espousal of their souls unto their only Saviour. I will as plainly, and as fully as I can, propose unto them the terms on which the glorious Redeemer would espouse them to Himself, in righteousness, judgment, and favor and mercies forever; and solicit their consent unto His proposals and overtures. Then would I go on, to do what may be expected from a tender parent for them, in their temporal circumstances."

# REFERENCES

[1] Spurgeon, Charles Haddon, as quoted on *Doug's Blog*, www.visionforum.com, (San Antonio, TX: The Vision Forum, Inc., 2003)

[2] Grant, George, article entitled *Father of the Founding Fathers*, (Franklin, TN: King's Meadow Study Center)

[3] Mather, Cotton, *A Father's Resolutions*, from the Cotton Mather Home Page, www.spurgeon.org/~phil/mather.htm, (Phillip R. Johnson, 2001), Preamble.

[4] Sproul, Jr., R.C., *When You Rise Up: A Covenantal Approach to Homeschooling*, (Phillipsburg, NJ: P&R Publishing Company, 2004), pp. 26-27.

[5] Sproul, Jr., p. 44.

[6] Phillips, Howard, as quoted by his son, Doug Phillips, during a conference entitled, *Your Gold to Refine*, presented by the Highlands Study Center, R.C. Sproul, Jr., Director, 2005.

[7] Miller, J.R., D.D., *Home-Making: What the Bible Says About Roles and Relationships in a Harmonious Christian Household*, (San Antonio, TX: The Vision Forum, Inc., 2003, Originally published 1882), pp. 140-141.

[8] Klicka, Christopher J., *Home Schooling, The Right Choice: An Academic, Historical, Practical, and Legal Perspective*, (Nashville, TN: Broadman & Holman Publishers, 2002), p. 51.

[9] Heaviside, Sheila; Rowand, Cassandra; Williams, Catrina & Farris, Elizabeth, *Violence and Discipline Problems in U.S. Public Schools: 1996-97*, (Washington DC: U.S. Department of Education, National Center for Educations Statistics, 1998), p. 67.

[10] Kurtz, Howard, *College Faculties a Most Liberal Lot, Study Finds*, (Washington DC: The Washington Post, March 29, 2005), p. C1.

---

[11] Ray, Brian D., Ph.D., *Home Educated and Now Adults: Their Community and Civic Involvement, Views About Homeschooling, and Other Traits,* (Salem, OR: NHERI Publications, 2004), p. 63.

[12] Boyd, Bob & Geri, from radio interview with Dr. Brian D. Ray on the Boyd's radio program, *Issues in Education,* as excerpted in the pamphlet, *Homeschoolers Grown Up: What Do the Facts Show?,* (Johnson City, TN: Homeschool Headquarters, 2004), p. 6.

[13] Ray, p. 41.

[14] Ray, p. 45.

[15] Seaman, Barrett, *Binge, What Your College Student Won't Tell You: Campus Life in an Age of Disconnection and Excess,* (Hoboken, NJ: John Wiley & Sons, Inc., 2005)

[16] Mather, Resolution 14.

[17] Sprague, William B., D.D., *Letters on Practical Subjects to a Daughter,* (Harrisonburg, VA: Sprinkle Publications, 1987), pp. 34-35.

[18] Brown, Jim, *Rampant Cheating Forces College to Change Honor Code,* AFA Online, source Agape Press, (Tupelo, MS: American Family Association, September 10, 2004)

[19] Mather, Preamble.

[20] Ray, p. 42.

[21] Ray, p. 44.

[22] Jayson, Sharon, *With 'Senioritis' the Diagnosis, the Search for a Cure is On: Experts See a Need for a Productive Bridge to College,* (McLean, VA: USA Today, April 19, 2005), p. 5D.

[23] Johnson, Frank, *Revenues and Expenditures for Public Elementary and Secondary Education: School Year 2002-03*, (Washington DC: National Center for Education Statistics, 2005), pp. 1-2.

[24] Fukuda-Parr, Sakiko, *Monitoring Human Development: Enlarging People's Choices*, (New York, NY: Human Development Report Office of the United Nations Development Programme, 2004), p. 150.

[25] Stoops, Nicole, *Educational Attainment in the United States: 2003*, (Washington DC: U.S. Census Bureau, 2004), p. 1.

[26] Mather, Resolution 18.

[27] Maxwell, Steven, *Preparing Sons to Provide for a Single-Income Family*, (Leavenworth, KS: Communication Concepts, Inc., 2001)

[28] Miller, p. 59.

[29] Murray, Andrew, *Raising Your Children for Christ*, (New Kensington, PA: Whitaker House, 1984), pp. 311-312.

[30] Murray, pp. 154-155.

[31] Miller, pp. 57-58.

[32] Mather, Resolution 18.

[33] Baum, Sandy & Payea, Kathleen, *Trends in College Pricing 2003*, (Washington DC: College Board Publications, 2004), p. 6.

[34] Baum, p. 10.

[35] Baum, p. 3.

[36] Baum, p. 3.

[37] Baum, Sandy & O'Malley, Marie, *College on Credit: How Borrowers Perceive Their Education Debt*, (Braintree, MA: Nellie Mae Corporation, February, 2003), p. v.

[38] Nellie Mae website, www.nelliemae.org, (Braintree, MA: Nellie Mae Corporation, 2004), Loan Center tab.

[39] Nichols, Stephen J., *Jonathan Edwards' Resolutions and Advice to Young Converts*, (Phillipsburg, NJ: P&R Publishing Company, 2001) p. 17.

[40] Nichols, pp. 6-8.

[41] Day, Jennifer Cheeseman & Newburger, Eric C., *The Big Payoff: Educational Attainment and Synthetic Estimates of Work-Life Earnings*, (Washington DC: U.S. Census Bureau, 2002), pp. 2-3.

[42] Oak Brook College of Law and Government Policy website, www.obcl.edu, (Fresno, CA: Oak Brook College, 2005), Statement of Mission page.

[43] Robinson, Jo Ann; Polite, Troy & Musick, Nancy, Editors, *2004-2005 National Guide to Educational Credit for Training Programs*, (Washington DC: American Council on Education, 2004), p. 2.

[44] Voeller, Brad, *Accelerated Distance Learning: The New Way to Earn Your College Degree in the Twenty-First Century*, (Hinsdale, IL: Dedicated Publishing, 2002), pp. 37-42.

[45] Thomas Edison State College website, www.tesc.edu, About Us tab.

[46] Excelsior College website, www.excelsior.edu, About Excelsior tab.

[47] Jordan, Stewart, *Catching God's Heart and Design*, (Huntsville, AL: available via his church's website at www.redeemerpca.org, 2002), p. 1.

[48] Sproul, Jr., pp. 27-28.

[49] Dodds, Elizabeth D., *Marriage to a Difficult Man: The Uncommon Union of Jonathan and Sarah Edwards*, (Laurel, MS: Audubon Press, 2003), pp. 31-32.

[50] Henry, Matthew, *Matthew Henry's Commentary on the Whole Bible*, available free of charge online at www.ccel.org/h/henry/mhc2, Jeremiah 6:16.

[51] Water, Mark, Compiler and Editor, *Parallel Commentary on the New Testament*, (Chattanooga, TN: AMG Publishers, 2003) pp. viii-ix.